THE JOURNAL OF

Poetry, Prose, & Visual Art

University of Colorado Anschutz Medical Campus

FRONT COVER ARTWORK
Chalk Art | Details of a Larger Vision

CAROLYN BREMER

BACK COVER ARTWORK
Drop the Ego

JULIETTE ORR

GRAPHIC DESIGN
Scott Allison
scottallisoncreative@gmail.com
ScottAllison.org

PRINTING
Bill Daley
Citizen Printing, Fort Collins
970.545.0699
BDaley@CitizenPrinting.com

Volume 9
2016

CONTENTS

PREFACE 7

A new home Heidi Tyrrell 8

Ordinary Carol H. Ehrlich 9

cadaver as first teacher Meha Semwal 10

the last rose Sally Peach 11

touch The Poet Spiel 12

Abuelita Adriana Romero 13

risus sardonicus Warren Martin Hern 14–15

The back nine Carol H. Ehrlich 16

The Medical Student Jeff Druck 17

In Death I live Fredrick Abrams 18–19

Death Bed Karen Leh 20

On White & the Symbolism of Coats Meha Semwal 21

Segundina and John Warren Martin Hern 22–23

Unexpected Visitor Fredrick Abrams 24

Celestial Fish at the Botanic Gardens Larry Allen 25

Sleeping Gypsy with Tiger Blanket, Homage to Henri Rousseau
John Bonath 26–27

The Sleeping Gypsy Henri Rousseau 26

Whirling Renaissance Michael Aubrey 28

Narcotic Shapeshifters Art Elser 29

The Players Anireddy Reddy 30–31

Lucy Gwen Frederick 32–33

The Dare Romany Redman 34–36

En Route to Emerald Lake | RMNP Carolyn Bremer 37

The Weight of Youth Rachael Ruff 38

Eclipse Over Portland Maine Kathleen Garrett 39

The Adult That You Are Carolyn Ho 40–42

You Can't Be Sick if You Don't Go to the Doctor Anonymous ... 43

In the Doctor's Waiting Room Art Elser 44

Marge Ian Neff 45

The Immigrant Mary Poole 46

Hug with a View April Netschke 47

Great Blue Heron-Everglades NP Patricia Nash 48

CONTENTS

A Guiding Light Huy Phan 49
High Seas Sally Preston 50
Soothsayer, soothe for S. Ian Neff 51
Blood and Flesh William Jensen 52–53
Forever, My Love Lisa R. Diaz 54–58
Predator's Gaze Ryan D'souza 59
The Dinner Mary Poole 60
Aspen Leaf George Ho, Jr. 61
Putting it into perspective: An inconvenience or a tragedy
Sharisse Arnold Rehring 62–63
diagram the heart Meha Semwal 64
heART flutters McKenzie Winter 65
Joan's Smile Stacey Wynne-Urbanowicz 66
Hangin' Out Michelle Alletag 67
Ginza Nights Huy Phan 68
Kauai sunset Patricia Nash 69
romancing the pain The Poet Spiel 70
Don't ever be an interesting patient Alexander Ghincea 71
Zusha Simon M. Kamau 72–73
Push Matthew Wood 74
Happening upon an Eastern fence lizard hatchling (Sceloporus undulates)
Rebecca Hollmann 75
The Land of Limbo Jean Abbott 76–77
The Death of My Patient Last Week L. A. Kahn 78–79
From: Animal Stories Jennie Hammet 80–83
Paul Jennie Hammett 84
Close Call David Weil 85
Buddha killed the Betta Michelle Colarelli 86–97
The Words Unspoken L. A. Kahn 88
To You Ryan Goffredi 89
The Universe Fredrick Abrams 90–91
The Sudden End of the Firefight Art Elser 92
Peeking in on the Downy Woodpecker (Picoides pubescens)
Rebecca Hollmann 93

CONTENTS

Art for Healing Steven Lewis 94

If I Was Good to You Christine Mitchell 95

Daffodil Anjali Dhurandhar 95

Spouting Rock Waterfall David Eckhardt 96

Untitled Elizabeth Swift 97

Diá del Juego James Engeln 98–100

Keep Climbing Nasser Alsaleh 101

It's All in Her Head Carol Calkins 102–103

Bangkok Oren M Gordon 104

Bones Rachael Ruff 105

on depression Sally Peach 106

Art for Healing Steven Lewis 107

Relaxing landscapes James Geyman 108

Great Blue Heron chasing away nest robbing cormorant
George Ho, Jr. 109

Workin' The Catapult Michael Aubrey 110

Two Pediatrics Stories in 55 Words Emily Hause 111

Goodbye-Hello Claire Ramirez 112

A Letter to My Guru Michael Himawan 113

She released a small cloud of telepathic butterflies... Oh my, oh my.
Brianna Smyk 114–116

True Happiness Adriana Romero 117

The Copier Eric Sasine 118–119

Dual Diagnosis Ligia Batista 120–121

Awaiting death James Yarovoy 122

Dance with me Warren Martin Hern 123

Rest now, little one Michelle Alletag 124

Mt. Evans David Weil 125

rhino Exit Sally Preston 126

Berlin Jennie Hammett 127

The Last Full Measure of Devotion Eric Sasine 128–129

Body remembers: Marlena Chertock 103–131

CONTRIBUTOR BIOGRAPHIES 132–143

ACKNOWLEDGEMENTS 144

Welcome to *The Human Touch* 2016—the annual anthology of prose, poetry, graphic art and photography created and contributed by the students, staff, faculty, alumni and friends of the University of Colorado Anschutz Medical Campus.

This volume is a celebration and showcase of the amazing talents and unique perspectives of our contributors, and we appreciate their support of and involvement in another stunning compilation of work. But behind the evocative words and compelling images is the commitment and creativity of our editors and board members. From inviting submissions to devising time lines to reviewing materials to working with graphic artists to endless proofreading, they devote many hours to producing the volume that you now hold in your hands. And they do all of this in addition to schedules packed with class meetings, study sessions, high-stakes exams, residency interviews and even internship duties! We are deeply grateful for their dedication and energy.

One of the biggest challenges of any literary and arts magazine is securing the necessary funding for the enterprise, no matter how big or small. We are extremely fortunate and especially thankful that Dr. Robert Anderson, Senior Associate Dean for Education, has committed to ongoing annual financial support for *The Human Touch*. This "gift" from the School of Medicine enables us to create what we hope is and will continue to be our "gift" to the community of the Anschutz Medical Campus: a beautifully rendered and emotionally powerful representation of the artistry and the diversity of our colleagues and friends.

We are, as always, thankful for the unwavering commitment and incredible generosity of Dr. Henry Claman to the Arts and Humanities in Healthcare Program. The program's mission is to realize the universal appeal of the arts and humanities and their power to connect student and teacher, patient and professional, citizen and artist, benefactor and institution. *The Human Touch* serves as a tangible means of making such connections.

Finally, on behalf of the editorial board, I want to thank and congratulate our 2016 Editors-in-Chief:

• Romany Redman, School of Medicine, Class of 2016
• Leslie Palacios-Helgeson, School of Medicine, Class of 2016

As noted, our editors have worked very hard over the past academic year and have produced a volume of which they (and we) can be very proud.

Therese (Tess) Jones, PhD
Director, Arts and Humanities in Healthcare Program

A new home

HEIDI TYRRELL

Rolling hills, shades of green and blue
billows of white caress peaks and hollars
giants stand beside her
She sits silently
Wormy chestnut somebody said
Gray, stripes of yellow, lines of age and weather
She is beautiful
her crown of metal dinged and dented
haven to the swallows in her eves
rain, hail, snow and sun adore and beat her
She is beautiful
timeless
She sits silently
She makes me smile

◆

Ordinary

CAROL H. EHRLICH

Just when I thought
we were too old for romance,
for the old fun that used to
tingle my spine and
tickle my innards—
just when I sighed,
settling, I guess, for a flat plate
of ordinary
for the rest of our days—
just then
I saw your smile,
felt your hand reach my shoulder,
touch my neck
in your old way of knowing.

In a transforming moment
the magic returned—
not the same,
but it tasted so sweet.
A slow-moving lightning
radiated through me.

Oh my…
a new, seasoned world began.

◆

cadaver as first teacher

MEHA SEMWAL

i used to think in wholes:
bones & muscle & fascia
indissectable but now, i keep

tally as my mind unravels,
catches too long on you
& your name, tries to ball

you up into my fist & purse
my lips *not to kiss but to set
sail:* i'm the waiting type,

the particles aching type,
the notches & landmarks
of my spine crumbling type

& for you i counted every vertebral
notch, your calcium fragments
in a box i couldn't quite

rebuild, no matter how much
i puzzled, how much the puzzle
wanted to unpuzzle itself, this toy

spinning top, this atlas of countries
& now skulls & now phantoms, asking
why the woman who doesn't see

is asking to be indivisible,
invisible to all your hellos
& unfarewells, i will learn

a new language, learn to slice skin
from viscera, *i'll split this scintillate,
touch your psoas, sacrum, scalp*

◆

the last rose

SALLY PEACH

when all the rest have gone,
      and the dust of frost beckons
              and mocks,
     she blossoms

her thorns are just a surface farce,
    hold her firmly,
           you'll forget them

petals like velvet—plush, lush—
  press, preserve, or
        she'll forget you

for she,
    the   rose of the season
      last
  won't

◆

touch

THE POET SPIEL

touching her
when she was dead
when i was certain
she could not speak
was a merciful dream
i could not before
have imagined

such pleasure
of her skin
her pure white hair
within my hands

i don't recall now
who took me away
to sign official papers
acknowledging
she was gone
the exact time
and was there
anything
i wished to claim

yes
a snip of hair
even now
i cannot think
of anything
so white
and yes
a few moments
alone with her
still warm
not resistant
her mouth
not suggesting
how i might
change my life
to suit her
◆

Previously published by *Chiron Review* 2004 and 2005,
Spiel, Pudding House chapbook, *it breathes on its own.*
©2003 Spiel

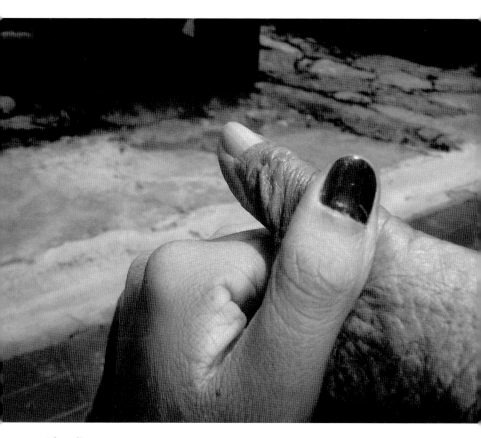

Abuelita

ADRIANA ROMERO

risus sardonicus

WARREN MARTIN HERN

black woman

    doctor

      walking brisklydowntheaisle

    between

     the

     two

     rows

     of

     beds

nodding and smiling
         into
            the

    isolation

      room

clouds of steam rolling out

a woman looked up sadly from a cradle to the

eyes of the physician

sharp

short

cry

stretchingviolentlymouthtwistingtoa

tortured sarcastic smilefrown

then

pucker

tremblejerk

the mother bent over the child speaking softly in

Ibo

and looked again at the younger

woman

we must try anyway said the doctor

◆

The back nine

CAROL H. EHRLICH

I travel the back nine
in a reverie,
absorbed in the sweet reward
of nearing completion,
all the time sorry to see the game end,
weighed down by the weary knowing
of shots hit wrong—
misjudged and just plain missed—
yet buoyed by the feeling still in my muscles of
playing well when sometimes I did.

I'd like to play it over,
to make the errors disappear,
to feel the good shots
once more ring true.
I'd like to wage it like a champion
and wear the triumph in my bones.

The truth is plain, however—
like a concert just over in a crowded hall,
like cycles of nature that never halt,
like the path of the sun,
the history is written.
It is what it is.

Do-overs are not an option.

◆

The Medical Student

JEFF DRUCK

Eager for Knowledge

physical exam, hard facts,

Compassion matters more

◆

In Death I live

FREDRICK ABRAMS

In memory the poet said one dies
yet is not dead
But I am gone as all have gone before
and after me will go
Yet know
I have a heart that I unlike the poet's metaphor
have truly left behind
Nor will it rest
but rather thrill again within another's chest
to live and love once more
And eyes for him
whose mind no more in vain
need struggle wistfully to retain
the images of his lifelong friend
to mend his vision
that he may see the glee
his grandchild feels who giggly tries
to blow the candles out
and leans to help
if need there be
I endure by yielding that
for which I have no need
My self has died before my cells you see
Spoken out the words have comic unreality
It's not a liver that I give but factory
for protein blocks
to build and feed a girl
who otherwise would waste away
But now she may arise
and simply walk in sun-drenched warmth
from azure skies
though I no longer may
Can anyone emancipate
from overt bonds of slavery a prisoner

more bound than he who
under penalty of death
must wrap himself in tubes and flasks
dialysis completes the task
of leaching out the toxic waste
when kidneys fail
I say in haste that my travail must pale
compared to that
my death releases him from jail
And more the child whose leg
a secret terror holds enfolds
a parasitic cancer growth that threatens
both his life and limb
What can my body do for him
A bone so surgeons make him whole
Replace a segment artfully
Then he can run the bases round
And cross home plate
as once I did
Unbound unfettered stands he upright
and I a kid again stand tall although
it cannot be
My self is gone and yet
I live in death
I still have much to give
By penchant I decry a waste
To those in haste to say, "We all must die"
I don't deny
that we are not to be repaired
for all eternity
Yet all the souls
whose lives I touch with freely given legacy
I know they will remember me
Remember me
Remember me
◆

Death Bed

KAREN LEH

The wife of my patient
is impatient.

Her mind is a wet newsprint.
She falls because
the earth cannot stop calling her.
His bones are eaten through.
He cannot lift his head.

She says, in a bullying voice,
"You'd better hurry and get well
because I need you for some things—

and I love you."

I am astonished,
but he says her name
and she hobbles to him.
His hand shakes
as he pulls her down
for a kiss.

I'm a butterfly then,
reading the air with its wings.

◆

On White & the Symbolism of Coats

MEHA SEMWAL

   I. i promise: you are not going to have to cut people open
  II. unless the surgeon overslept & they all look at you,
horror & confusion in their eyes
 III. *you're the only one,* they'll say
 IV. soaped & gloved & masked like a B-list film,
you will then have to cut people open
  V. *he's flatlining!*
 VI. they'll say this in a flatlining voice
VII. the friend who looks at your earlobe when you speak
is unimpressed as you suture
VIII. three complications & a hematoma later, you fall asleep
 IX. at the wheel, which is a needle, which is a scalpel, which is a gun:
they all go off like alarms, instruments of experimental deceit
& unrelenting power, you hold them gingerly, tell the others to
stand back! give us some air! as though you were a real
  X. doctor(ed) excuse
 XI. for a resident, trumped up & trawling, a bottom-feeder,
a bristleworming sea snail
XII. what will they do with me? *i want to swallow the stars,
one by one, through a straw*
    ◆

Segundina and John

WARREN MARTIN HERN

About a week after I arrived in the village, Segundina died. Rosalina was one of her daughters. I had been called to Segundina's house the day after I arrived because she was very ill. Segundina, a woman of about 75 or 80, could no longer walk. She was lying under a mosquito net on a straw mat on the ground. Her family had placed a lot of fine river sand all around her bed since she could not walk to the bushes to "hacer su necesidad." Her grandchildren brought her food and clean sand. She was in pain from her bones. Julio thought she had cancer of some kind. She also had tuberculosis. By now she had edema in her legs, probably from congestive heart failure because it developed in her arms, also, within a few days. She itched all over. I thought she also might have kidney failure. There were always three or four family members waiting on the floor of the kitchen by her mosquito net. Sometimes she would sit up and eat a little. Then she couldn't sit.

She moaned with pain and moved to escape it. With the little medicine I had, there was not much I could do except to try to make her comfortable.

Finally, one morning, a wail went up from that part of the village. Segundina had died. Her daughters, female cousins, and granddaughters gathered by her corpse, now wrapped in handspun cloth, to wail. Rosalina was there with her sisters. The women covered their heads with dark shawls and sat cross-legged along the edge of the kitchen. They wailed the Shipibo death song, a minor key, ringing with sadness, and the words gave tribute to their mother, aunt, cousin, as she was to them. Segundina's grandsons made a casket from a canoe. That afternoon, they took her to the cemetery.

I could not help comparing the death of Segundina, who died with her family and friends gathered by her for the final vigil around the clock—they knew death was approaching—to the death of my father, who died several years ago in a local hospital, well attended by the Intensive Care Unit crew, but without his friends. Here was a man who had thousands of friends who would do anything for him and loved him, and who had a family who loved him, but who died virtually alone, who faced the terror of death without someone he loved close by his side all the time. We could not know that this was the time because we had pulled him back from the brink so many times; my sisters could not be there each visit to the abyss because they lived so far away, my mother was incapacitated from a serious injury, and I was attending my own patients, whom I could not leave. I could only call the hospital between each of them. He's getting air better. His oxygen saturation is up. We just moved him to ICU. He's holding his own. He's comfortable.

He opened his eyes with all his effort to look at me when I got there, but he couldn't talk with all the tubes. He nodded a little. And then he sank. The line between life and death became not a last breath but a glowing green line on a glass screen. There was no wailing, but there was no one to hear. Death came alone.

When I wheeled my mother in to see him, he was gone. The ICU people had tried and tried, but it was no use. They were removing the tubes, the artificial veins and sinews, our equivalent to the Shipibo <u>hanshítote wiwa!</u>, the "song by which we hold back death," but there was no medicine man to sing that beautiful melancholy minor chant, no silent kinsmen gathered around to sit on the old overturned canoe and share our grief, only the sound of electronic monitors humming along without a stimulus or response in the ether out there. He was gone. He was at peace. And we couldn't get him back. The end of life was bandaged in wires and curtains.

My mother pulled herself up from the wheelchair and, ever so gently touching his face, leaned over and kissed him. "Johnny," she said. After awhile, we left.

For us, there was pain without a wound.

◆

Unexpected Visitor

FREDRICK ABRAMS

Lying still in a cone like the eye of a hurricane
More in vacuum than in peace
Life ebbing with throbbing sounds

The physical senses distant
The cold sweat
Not so cold as your mortality pressing upon you
You're undone
You've left things undone
Goodbyes unsaid

Black wings and the whining of a dynamo
Familiar things shimmering
As though they were seen through the
Heat of midday
And a sense of unavailing despair
No next times
All the next times used up

◆

Celestial Fish at the Botanic Gardens

LARRY ALLEN

Sleeping Gypsy with Tiger Blanket,
Homage to Henri Rousseau Photograph above and at right

JOHN BONATH

The Sleeping Gypsy

HENRI ROUSSEAU, 1897, Color on canvas, 130 cm x 201 cm
Original painting located at Museum of Modern Art, New York, NY

*This diptych represents a
more complete portrait of
a homeless man than each
single image could alone.*

– JOHN BONATH

Whirling Renaissance

MICHAEL AUBREY

Narcotic Shapeshifters

ART ELSER

I sit in my hospital bed and watch a squadron
of silver shapeshifters fly out of the room
and stop behind the nurses' station. There
they form precise ranks as they pass in review
and then hover in flights ready for a mission.
I send my wife and kids out to look at them,
but they are unable to see them. They shake
their heads and look at me as if I'm crazy.
Another line of larger shapes drifts
into my room and lands on the ceiling
to form baroque patterns that look
like streets in some futuristic city.

Later that evening, the night nurse
comes into the room, and I show her
the detailed patterns on the ceiling
and the flight of large metallic shapes
flying in to create intricate patterns.
She does not see them either, so I have her
come close to the bed where I can point
to the patterns. Again, she doesn't see them.
But unlike my family, she looks at me
with knowing concern and tells me that I
am hallucinating from the anesthesia and drugs
the doctors have given me over the past week.

I'm dismayed that the shapes are phantoms
of my drugged mind. But I sit back, smile,
and enjoy the magic air show.

◆

The Players

ANIREDDY REDDY

Sir William Osler once said, "A physician sits in the front row of the theater of life."
He was wrong.
A physician is a player in the theater of life.

The sound of a helicopter heralds her arrival.

She has quite the welcoming party. The apprehension is palpable
as the players assemble: nurses, residents, fellows, and attendings cast
from the ICU, gastroenterology, surgery, cardiology… the list continues
to grow, maybe twenty-five in all. At any other time, her room would
have been a comical comparison to a packed clown car; so many players
there are. Each gathers with a tense exchange of words, finding their
place on the stage, waiting.

She rolls quietly down the hallway, all 20 pounds of her.

An uncharacteristic silence falls as wires are disconnected and
reconnected, her tiny body transferred from one bed to another.
Once moved, the players exhale the smallest sigh of relief, for this
was a minor, yet significant success.

And then she coughed the slightest cough, barely perceptible to
the human ear.

But it was visible to the eye. Blood bubbles forth, pouring
from her mouth, collecting around her soft face.

The players spring to action and suddenly there is no silence.
There is a call for trauma blood…fluids…pressors…labs…more blood…
to the backdrop of a heart that speeds, but pumps fruitlessly.

The players line up, thrusting unholy adult weight on this frail body.
That is what this stage requires and the players fight admirably. They
have been trained well, to keep a heart beating that is broken.

Her mother is somehow at the nurse's station–how did she get there? She is wailing a deep sound, as if her body is trying to purge an evil that clings too tightly.

After hours of blood and pumping, she is stably unstable, in need of an operating room and sterile, definitive action.

Her parents request to touch her as she rolls towards the OR, amidst the grand caravan of players and props that accompany her. A request not usually granted except that it may be the last.

She passes, not unexpectedly, during surgery. They find it in the subclavian artery. Perhaps it came from a hearing aid or singing birthday card. No bigger than a dime, but much more costly, carving a devastating path from esophagus to aorta.

Her chances were small if anything, but the work of the players was still worthy.

They do not play God, but they play hope. They are staunch defenders of life and you shall not pass from one world to another until they have taken to the stage. Until they have concentrated centuries of knowledge and years of practice into near magic, in an attempt to change fate…

…or at least create space for goodbye.

These are the players.

And I want to be one.

◆

This story documents a case of an 18-month-old female who swallowed a button battery, a rare, but deadly pediatric ingestion.

Lucy

GWEN FREDERICK

I lost my cocker spaniel, Teddybear, when he was 15 ½. He was my one and only dog I'd wanted all my life. My aunt raised cockers when we were growing up and I'd always loved them because they're so soft and cuddly. Like a Teddy Bear. I got Teddy to get me off the couch. I was depressed after my divorce and not having any children. I believe he saved my life. I had to get up and take him for a walk, so I was getting fresh air and seeing nature and not sitting around thinking.

Toward the end, he had so many problems from old age, but he just kept hanging in there. A friend of mine said Teddy didn't want to leave me. It took me a long time to decide to have him put to sleep. It broke my heart, but I had read something about how to make that difficult decision. It said they've depended on us their whole life to make decisions for them and this is the last loving thing we can do for them. I had decided long before that the only thing that would make up for losing Teddy would be to rescue a dog that needed a home.

I had seen this sweet looking dog named Lucy on the Rocky Mountain Cocker Rescue website site for quite a few months. She was partially blind from inbreeding, it said. She had come from an Amish puppymill in Missouri and only had one pup at a time, so I guess they didn't want her. And she was a cocker spaniel mix. They thought she was part Cavalier King Charles Spaniel. I wasn't sure about this, but made arrangements to meet Lucy. It wasn't love at first sight as I was a little scared to get a sight-impaired dog. It was hard to connect because she was so timid. I didn't want to lose her, but I had to go home and think about it. Could I learn to love her as much as I had Teddy?

Her foster family had taken good care of her and taught her some commands. Her foster mom had told me all about her. She was a good dog after all she'd been through. We were a good match. Lucy needed a quiet home without children or lots going on. I wanted her and was ready to do whatever it took to make her happy. She is no trouble at all. She can see some movement and shadows. She doesn't run into the furniture or anything.

As it turned out, she was the most affectionate dog I'd ever seen. When she felt safe on the couch, she just wanted to be loved and hugged and petted. She couldn't get enough. When you stop petting her even for a second, she ever so lightly touches her paw to your arm to say, "Don't stop!" When I told my sister that, she said, "Well, she's in the right place.' I wanted a dog I could cuddle with and I got it. She has not barked once, but howls when the phone rings. Puppymill dogs usually don't know how to play. I buy her toys, but she can't see to chase a ball and she doesn't care about them. And she doesn't chase squirrels because she can't see them; so that's a bonus.

I took Lucy to an eye specialist to tell me exactly what's going on with her eyes. She has something called Asteroid Hyalosis. When you shine a light in in her eyes, you see beautiful and sparkly silver things. A friend told me St. Lucy is the patron saint of the blind and sight impaired.

But she seems to get along perfectly fine without her sight. A dog's main senses are their hearing and smell anyway. She trots ahead of me when we go for walks like she's not afraid of anything. She's scared of loud noises like most dogs. She was afraid to go into the kitchen and acted like she was going to fall into a hole if she stepped onto the white linoleum. I have a rug there for her now which helps.

I talk to her a lot because of her not being able to see. I decided since she can't see me, I want her to always know that I see her. I have learned many things from Lucy. I've learned to have faith and courage even when I'm not sure what's ahead. I've learned not to make a big deal out of imagined problems. I've learned to be brave and assume the best will happen. And that I'm being taken care of even when it doesn't always feel like it. There are a lot of scary things in life, but if I charge ahead and have faith, I will be ok. I have faith the floor will be there when I step on it.

◆

The Dare

ROMANY REDMAN

The first thing you see is a raskolnikov face, split by a deep scar running diagonally from the sunken eye hiding under furrowed brow to the turned down corner of colorless mouth. Your gaze moves on reading the novel of crime and punishment in blue-green ink from neck to knuckles wrapped around clenched fists. Even with the extra shirt, ribs protrude through, giving the strangely familiar illusion of a wind-beaten tarp draped over empty scaffolding. An abandoned construction site. The bricks ran out.

You make your introductions, consents, the recorder clicks on, and his story begins.

"I have had tuberculosis for seventeen years."

...

"What more is there to tell?! Seventeen f@#$ing years!"

The conversation pauses for a pseudo-coughing fit, aimed vindictively at your flimsy paper face mask. It is the same mask you have kept folded in the pocket of your whites since the jaunt further up the dirt road into the forest when you visited the closed pediatric ward last month. You make a mental note to wear two pairs of socks tomorrow. That way you can slightly more comfortably queue at the post office and inquire if that box of N-95 respirators you had sent from Moscow last fall has arrived yet.

The tale continues reluctantly. Bit by bit, the anecdotes start to weave a larger picture, a portrait of either a man or his disease. It is still too soon to tell. The price of each piece of plot is a massive dose of anger. At progressively louder volumes.

No trouble there. You are angry too. At the same things. So it all brushes off more readily than snowflakes from mittened hands. Some sly segues later, and the recorder is still running.

Anger is still running. Despite growing energy expenditure with each inflammatory exhalation from across the table, despite reciprocal heat escaping your knitted collar, the examination room is frigid. The saga ultimately ends with arms out-stretched in a giant shrug and stone-cold certainty proclaiming,
 "The world has forsaken me."

...

Shit.

Now it is your turn to pause the conversation. Your sniffling nose has gone overboard. Coughing too. The mask comes off, and you reach for a tissue to wipe away the snot. Some blood marks the thin paper, probably from those raw sinuses parched in the dry Siberian winter skies. Your mind once again exits the narrative to make another mental note: Check with Sasha when the repairs finish, and schedule your imaging once the radiology department resumes their work in the future.

You resume your work in the present. Your nose resumes its Neva. Anger resumes.

Anger about poverty, inequalities, and social determinants of health. Anger at gray walls and gray porridge. Anger about there being more tubercular thoracic surgeons on staff than phthisiology internists. Anger that last week you let slip about some Global Fund politics and access to second-line drugs during an interview, and a young man chose to lose a lung – a lung! – rather than sit through eighteen more months of uncertain therapy. Anger that some cases are quarantined away in the woods out of sight not even for their own good and hardly anyone else's. Anger that scarred lungs and tattooed arms mean more than loving hearts or pained souls. Anger at incarceration, debilitating psychiatric illness, and lousy, dust-filled jobs. Anger at fake papers, crippling migration, and economic refugeeism. Anger at heroin, alcohol, and the sorrows that put the bottle on the table. Anger about ototoxicity, orange tears, and no other options. Anger ad nauseam.

The anger, the snot, the pounding headache. You need some air.

But air comes at a premium here.

Take shallow breaths. Outside awaits only that cold-induced bronchospasm that arose from waiting at bus stops too long.

—
continued on next page...

Take shallow breaths.

Take your puny shallow breaths and think your shallow thoughts. Thoughts about how the person needing air here is you. Worry about your cough and your bloody tissue. Breathe shallow and worry about your work. Pull the truth like taffy from stories told and code into clear-cut categories the dodecahedral dimensions of another universe, another human being. Breathe shallow and contemplate coping with your mantle of willing witness. Suffer, but only secondhand. Your self-imposed quarantine ends routinely at five PM. Breathe shallow and fear that your subclinical PTSD will not sit calmly behind a curtain of avoidance or snuggle down in a box labeled 'vicarious trauma' and tie itself up with a bow. Toy with apprehension about your ability to cope with anything. Because it is your coping that counts, your trauma that matters. Breathe shallow and measure hypersensitive survivor's guilt against gritty stoicism of stubborn hope, each alternatively a sign of weak-ness or of human-ness. Or both. Ponder how it is that after months of listening to numerous protracted tales of woe, your skin has simultaneously toughened up and worn so very thin.

And this sallow scowl across the table has the audacity and veracity to pepper holes in what remains of your oh so fragile skin. To shower stinging barbs of bitter truth. To self-righteously use these last moments of prolonged, violent death to prove your despicableness. To exercise last powers as a living human being to peer through empty wells of eyes that, like a paired magnifying glass poised on a frantic ant, aim to incinerate in retribution your last feeble, rickety, writhing strand of compassion.

Yet in a grand inquisition of dostoyevskian proportions, those same vacant eyes implore you to find the essence of humanity hiding in their depths. His humanity, your humanity. Find it. Do not lose it. Do not let it calcify into stone or cavitate into a dark void or disseminate into nothingness.

After one last convulsive cough, your flimsy mask is back in its place, tucked around your ears and resting over the bridge of your nose. Saving face.

The mask nods acknowledgement, the world has forsaken you. The recorder clicks off. Your eyes fall to the floor, and you watch a shadow of a man pass on through the door.

The footsteps fade, but your ears are still ringing with silent echoes of voices. Could it be?! Yes, your voice and his voice shouting at each other from across the valley, shouting in unison:
"I have not forsaken you".

◆

En Route to Emerald Lake | RMNP

CAROLYN BREMER

The Weight of Youth

RACHAEL RUFF

It starts with contemplation.
With an image in the distance
so fuzzy and far away that it
is hardly even a concept.

Years later, it still percolates
in the back of the mind.
More solid and more near.
There is some understanding
of what was and what could be.
But potential broods when unused.

If only it could be brought
from the mind and into reality.
It seems so close, with real
mass that can be captured and
held. But nothing quite satisfies.

By the time you can actually see it,
grasp it in the palm of your hand,
you realize it has become much
too heavy for you to bear.

◆

Eclipse Over Portland Maine

KATHLEEN GARRETT

In Eastern Park on Congress Square
I find the perfect view
As seven sisters serenade a rising Hunter's Moon
Not red with blood but Mesa Mud
A ruddy desert hue
An orb of dust detained as such
On the sole of a traveler's shoe
Down East delight obsidian night
My dreams safe with a friend
Whose wizened eyes record the skies
To guide me home again;
But not tonight—in obscure light
No, I'll wait here at the crossing
With the moon per chance in a soft slow dance
On the eve of a winter's frosting
◆

The Adult That You Are

CAROLYN HO

It's funny how life works
How unpredictable it is
So many simple things
Often come out of nowhere
Irritating and inconvenient

The same can be said of pain
It never hits when you expect it to
When you're prepared

It doesn't start with that one phone call
With the words "He's gone"

No, it started two years ago
With a startling ring in the middle of the night
Announcing the presence of cancers
Spread across a frail body
Leaving behind a blazing trail
That could only end in hopelessness

The pain in that moment was sharp
Burning even
Laced with a sour hint of fear
"How much time does he have?"
"A few months, maybe more"

And when that time actually came
When you picked up that call
That was just slightly off schedule
Because being the adult that you are
You kept track of such things
And being the adult that you are,
You were prepared for the inevitable

But, it never came
Even as the truth washed over you
Details on the funeral, family, and visiting relatives
Were easily accepted
You were fine, calm even

And with your logical mind
You thought of the maturity and growth
That allowed you to accept his death
That allowed you to accept the last two years
That allowed you to move on
And being the adult that you are
The grief could not touch you anymore
It was over

And so you never saw it coming
When it snuck up on you weeks later
As you walked down the store aisle
And caught sight of a toy car
That's when the memories came flooding
Of the time he gave you your first mini racecar
Of the arguments later on and the frustration
Of how you said you'd see him again at Christmas
Of how he no longer recognized you the last time you called
And then of the face that you no longer recognized in the coffin

—

continued on next page...

You thought you were over it
But there it was
Clamping up your throat
Burning behind your eyes
And you feel a hand at your shoulder
Hear a voice behind you
"Are you alright?"
A pause, then a smile
"Just a crazy day. Thanks"
A goodbye
And then you turn away
One step, then another
One breath, and then another
As you walk casually past the exit
Then enter your car

And when the tears come streaming
You shut your eyes and clench your jaw
Pretending that this wasn't happening
Because you were supposed to have been over it
Because you are an adult
And you clung to that word
A mantra, a shield, a prayer
Because without it, you would drown
Without it, you would have to face reality
Face the truth
So, you wipe your eyes
Take a deep breath
And pretend it never happened
As you drive off
Like the adult that you are

◆

You Can't Be Sick if You Don't Go to the Doctor

ANONYMOUS

Paper jacket, open in front.
Paper drape.
Paper covering on the exam table.
I feel like a piece of gristle someone spat into a napkin.

Knock knock. The doctor and nurse come in.
The doctor says they can get me a blanket if I'm cold. I say let's get this over with.

It's my favorite day of the year, I say, the words soaked with sarcasm.
I apologize, it's nothing personal.
I add, if it's true what they say about doctors being bad patients,
then I'm half-way there.

Legs up, drape up, insert that, swipe there, swab in jar.
Non-offensive chit chat about the weather.

Next. Palpate the left side. The lymph nodes tickle.
Palpate the right side.

He stops.

What's wrong I ask.
You feel that, he says.
Feel WHAT.

And there it is.

It's probably a cyst he says, but I'll put the order in for a mammogram to be sure.
Okay, I say.

He orders a CBC and I don't flinch as the nurse inserts the needle.
She asks what kind of doctor I want to be.
I think, a LIVE one.

Surgeon, I say.

It's my favorite day of the year.

◆

In the Doctor's Waiting Room

ART ELSER

A short, dark-haired woman in her late sixties, in a red jacket,
leads her husband in and settles him in a chair.
She chats briefly with the receptionist,
her small hands flitting.
She sits down ninety degrees to her husband, watching over him.
They settle quietly, his long, thin white cane held at the ready
in his fleshy left hand.
His right hand rests on his knee and moves nervously
as if finding a message there in braille.

Another couple, also short and stocky, twenty years younger,
appears. The man whispers to the red jacket and sits.
He takes a car magazine offered by his wife.
She reads a medical magazine.
He unzips his leather jacket,
flips through pages,
scarcely looking at the pictures,
hunching over until his jacket resembles
the shell of a turtle.

His wife nervously scans her magazine, until she finds something,
and whispers urgently to him.
He pulls away and waves a pudgy hand at her with a short flick
of the wrist to stop her whispering.
She reads anyway,
symptoms of Parkinson's disease.
Prognosis—no cure.
Treatment—none that lasts.

A nurse calls the older couple,
they rise, joined by their son.
The young wife fidgets,
sure she already knows what they are about to learn.

◆

Marge

IAN NEFF

i said
happy Thanksgiving day

&

she said
it's just another thanksgiving day.

&

i felt the lowercaseness of her smile

◆

The Immigrant

MARY POOLE

Is there room for me in your school, your church, your neighborhood?

Is there room for me in your business, your hospital, university?

Is there room for me in your town, your state, your country?

There is no room for me.

◆

Hug with a View

APRIL NETSCHKE

Great Blue Heron-Everglades NP

PATRICIA NASH

A Guiding Light

HUY PHAN

High Seas

SALLY PRESTON

Soothsayer, soothe
for S.

IAN NEFF

slender, then unpacked
this breath expands to fit a room

human entrails could uncoil
& lead twenty feet in any direction
without saying where to go
any better than a witch's goat's liver

your father, your mother, entombed
at the bottom
of river-canyon folds of cortex

in which gorge & how far down
to their memory & where did you get lost

no one can say if they called or not
& so you wait

i cannot say how much space
a brain would cover
stretched out & flattened
if the convolutions could carpet a living room
or merely cover a table at dinner time

i do not know how far you must go
to meet your mother
only that she is not coming here

◆

Blood and Flesh

WILLIAM JENSEN

The meaning of life is found in revelation, a revelation that is present in each one of us. To be found where our blood and flesh whisper to our unconscious.

Dr. George Sheehan
Running and Being

The blood and flesh of patients speak to my unconscious. Sometimes it is a whisper, other times a scream. But their blood and flesh remind me of my own–my own humanity and mortality. This reminder is a revelation of the life and death present within me.

When I started as a chaplain, I covered cardiac units. I saw patients who were decades older than me come in for a cath or meds or a CABG. But it wasn't until I saw a patient come in who was about my age that my mortality came up and slapped me in the face. I reacted–stopped putting salt on anything and started taking the stairs everywhere, even up to my unit on the 9th floor. I'd show up sweaty and out of breath. I felt fragile.

I am surrounded by mortality. Whether a result of bad decisions, bad genes or bad luck, it destabilizes me. It has a cumulative effect. It shows up from time to time, sometimes in unexpected places. I see myself in a patient, or an elderly woman reminds me of grandma Jiny when she died. Adult children with aging parents give a window into the future, and the trauma of accidents and diagnoses remind me of how tenuous my hold on my life really is. Then seeing parents grieve the death of a child opens a hell I am scared to even consider.

I don't have a solution. I haven't found a way to be with people who are sick, suffering, and dying without being impacted. Their blood and flesh speak to me and remind me that I'm not that different.

My faith gives me hope, but it does not take away the darkness that can emerge during family meetings or on the way home from work. I'm tempted to pull back, to try to focus on safer or happier things. Yet I have learned that when this darkness arises, I should not run from it. I should not try to leave the room or change the subject. Instead, I should welcome the revelation–the flesh and blood connection it creates between us. It can be a moment of grief and fear, but it can also be a moment of strength and love. And sometimes even beauty.

While I can feel very sad, I am also very grateful. Grateful to do this work–to be entrusted with the care of another human being, and at such a critical moment in life. Grateful to work with wonderful people who love and support me. And grateful for my life and family and friends.

The quote says that the meaning of life is found in revelation. I find this to be true. The blood and flesh of patients speak to me. The message is often hard and sad and dark, and reminds me that I am also blood and flesh. That their mortality and mine are not that different. This is a hard reminder that can stop me cold in the middle of a busy day.

Sometimes it comes as a whisper, and sometimes a scream. But this reminder is a revelation of not only the death, but also of the life present within me. And no matter how hard it can be, I hope I never come to the point that I stop listening.

◆

Forever, My Love

LISA R. DIAZ

The security line at LAX was moving slower than usual today. Anna Frankel looked to the front of the shoeless line of passengers, wondering if she would miss her flight. The possibility was both stressful and a relief.

Then it happened. The familiar sound that always returned Anna to a childhood memory, so many years ago. A well-dressed passenger juggling his shiny black oxfords, wool overcoat and jewelry while waiting for the security scan was standing in front of her and dropped his perfectly round golden wedding band on the hard floor of the security checkpoint … Clink! Rollllllllll. Stop… that familiar sound.

Anna closed her eyes and reflected on a moment from 75 years ago, when the same sound, clink, rolllllllllll, stop changed everything about her life's meaning. This was a reminder of the truth she wished that she never knew, because it defined a lifetime she survived, because of something terrible and unforgivable that happened. Something that she did not do, yet she still felt horribly responsible for all of it.

Anna looked down, and realized that the ring had landed next to her stocking-covered toe. After uncomfortable smiles with the stranger, an awkward joint effort to bend over and retrieve the ring, two abrupt and polite declarations of "excuse-me," the incident was over, and they could both move on to the security task at hand.

Anna reached into her jacket pocket and grasped her ring, which she has been keeping in her coat pocket for 75 years, fidgeting with its smooth, perfect shape until she felt calm again. Whenever she fidgeted with the ring, Anna would always reflect upon the ring's Polish inscription, "Zawsze, moja miłość." (pronounced, "zavsheh moya meewosht"). She avoided learning what the words meant. Learning the meaning meant getting too close to the truth behind the ring.

Anna recalled that moment in the kitchen, when she was only 7 years old in Munich. Clink, rolllllllllll, stop. The phantom sound would not leave her alone. A reminder that this journey to New York should have happened long ago had Anna been brave enough. After finding the granddaughter of the ring's owner, Anna planned this trip in her mind at least a dozen times. Now, at 82 years old, this journey MUST HAPPEN. Not next year. NOW.

Reflecting back to 1940, Anna remembered the day that her father came home with his medical bag, as he always did, placing it on the kitchen table and retreating to his nightly shower. She was always a very curious little girl, and decided to see what was inside this oversized and weather-worn black leather bag. Quietly opening the bag, she pulled the contents out and gingerly placed each item on the table so no one would hear her. A few personal medical tools, a pocket neatly cradled some papers and a pen. Tucked amongst the papers were several labeled envelopes. Anna carefully removed one of the envelopes that was unsealed with the label, "Sasha Schwartz - Polin"("Polish" in German). Her curiosity piqued, Anna tipped the envelope to take a quick peek inside. But as she tipped the envelope, she was startled by the sound of something dropping out of the envelope and falling to the floor. Clink, rolllllllllll, stop. A gold wedding band dropped to the floor, rolled a bit and then stopped just before hiding under the stove. As she heard her mother returning to the kitchen, Anna hastily returned the items to the bag. Her mother returned to the kitchen before Anna could get the ring back in its proper place. Panicking, Anna picked up the wedding band and hid it in her pocket.

continued on next page...

That night, Anna examined the ring while lying in bed. A full moon softly lit her bedroom just enough to be able to examine the ring, a simple gold band, somewhat worn, but very smooth. Inside the band, a Polish inscription read, "Zawsze, moja miłość". Anna did not know what the inscription meant, but she kept repeating it in her mind, silently mispronouncing the words with her German accent. She fell asleep to the sounds of those words that night, imagining what they could mean and feeling a bit naughty for keeping something that probably belonged to someone else. Anna knew that if she returned the ring to her father, her curiosity in the kitchen would be revealed, and she would likely be punished for her actions.

The four-hour flight from Los Angeles to New York felt like 30 minutes. Anna recalled the phone call to Rhonda in Brooklyn, the woman she was flying across the country to meet.

"Hello, is this Rhonda Stein? My name is Anna Frankel. I have something that belonged to your grandmother, Sasha Schwartz. I'd rather explain in person, if you don't mind… I'd like to visit you and return it… I can fly to New York next week… OK. I will see you then." Anna wondered how Rhonda would react to her story. A lifetime of guilt for the sins of her father. The sins that kept Anna and her family alive in exchange for the millions that did not survive. The decision her father made to choose life for his family in exchange for the work he was ordered to complete in the name of surgical research for the Third Reich, as a Nazi physician, conducting medical experiments on Polish Jews. But her father agreed to do it. And that was the inner conflict she could not resolve.

During the war, Anna never knew what her father did. He always came home full of love. Sometimes smiling, and sometimes straight-faced and exhausted. It was 10 years later, long after Anna and her mother were settled into their American life, that she found the letter from Anna's father to her mother, begging forgiveness while awaiting trial for his crimes.

That was when the ring,
found in an innocent envelope,
in her childhood home,
in the kitchen,
when no one was looking,
changed from a good luck charm to a foreign yet familiar object that imprisoned her in a shadow of darkness. The truth was hideous and sickened her. She moved through life on autopilot—doing all the right things while struggling to be close to anyone who entered her life, including her husband Edward, who knew nothing of this part of her family history.

Keeping the ring in her pocket was a compulsive form of security. Any time something awkward or stressful happened, she would hold the ring and rotate her thumb gently around its smooth, golden circumference, until she felt better. She would say the words from the inscription silently in her mind with the same mispronounced German accent attempting the Polish phrase, "Zawsze, moja miłość."

As Anna headed up the walkway to Rhonda Stein's Brooklyn brownstone, she held the ring in her pocket. Before she got to the doorstep, the front door opened, startling Anna.

A welcoming voice from a woman, mid 40s, tall, lean, with a common yet warm expression who smiled and announced, "You must be Anna Frankel! Welcome! I hope your trip to New York was comfortable."

"Hello! Thank you. Yes, it was." What to say next? Anna's staccato reply felt awkward.

"Please come in! May I offer you some tea?"

—
continued on next page...

Anna stepped inside. The brownstone felt bright and warm. In the entry, hung an old black and white photo of a couple. The photo appeared to be from the 30s, judging by the clothing they wore. Below the photo hung an embroidered heirloom piece displayed in a frame, with those familiar words, Zawsze, moja miłość.

Anna looked closely at the embroidery and the photo. "That's very nice."

"You must recognize my grandmother with my grandfather. It's their wedding picture!"

"Ahh." Anna did not want to admit that she never actually saw or met Rhonda's grandmother. "What does the embroidery say?"
Rhonda read the inscription speaking perfect Polish, "'Zawsze, moja miłość.' It means, 'Forever, my love.' My mother told me that it was a special saying between my grandparents. They said it to my mother when she was little, and then to each other every night before going to bed. I never met my grandmother, so this expression calms me and helps me feel connected to her on some level."

Anna closed her eyes, let go of the ring in her pocket, took a deep breath, and replied, "That expression calms me too. And yes, please, I'd love some tea."

Anna Frankel sat down in Rhonda Stein's modest Brooklyn living room, and began the journey of reconciling her own life and the memory of a Polish woman she never met, but whose love for her family endured the test of time.

◆

Predator's Gaze

RYAN D'SOUZA

The Dinner

MARY POOLE

I was handed a cup of darkness
Served on a saucer of guilt.
The table was set with sadness,
Knives sharpened with regret.
Recriminations spilled from the pitcher
Staining the cloth with remorse.
A helping of pity and anguish
Garnished with skewers of loss.
I drank of the cup of darkness
Saw dregs of destruction and pain.
All hope for redemption abandoned,
I left the table in shame.

◆

Aspen Leaf

GEORGE HO, JR.

Spring brings life back to the aspen tree
Tender green leaves emerge
As the sun warms the air and the earth
Liquid and nourishment flow from the leafstalk to the veins
The leaf grows, enlarges with deepening green
Shaped like a swollen hybrid of a spade and a heart
Each leaf shades and competes with its neighbors for the sun's ray
Converts carbon dioxide to oxygen through photosynthesis
Gentle breeze sets the leaves to flutter and tremble, elbowing each other
Frolicking and warming up to rhythmic shimmy
And quake with greater intensity
When the wind blows a stronger gust
Vying to see who can excel in rhythm, frequency and form
Baring shamelessly the lighter underside with synchronous motion of the quivering
Breathtaking and breathless as the gust swirls and howls
Calming to stillness and silence as the wind abates
Dew collects as the night air cools
Washes off the dust baked on by the sun
Rain, sleet and occasional hail assault the leaves
Cleansing them as the dew
The cycle repeats and repeats until Fall descends
Shortened days and cooler nights signal a change
Youthful leaves become thicker and darker green over Summer months
Now, change yet again, as flow in the leafstalk slows, then ceases
Green turns light yellow deepening to golden and dark brown
The texture matures from succulent and tender
To rough and tough, then
To dried and crisp in the end
The cycle of the now unrecognizable leaf is complete
With the next gust of wind, it sails off with its siblings without a quiver
Landing near or far from the mother tree
Then, begins to decay over the long Winter to reunite with Mother Earth

◆

Putting it into perspective:
An inconvenience or a tragedy

SHARISSE ARNOLD REHRING

It was mid-afternoon, and in the midst of my busy day of patient care, my cell phone rang. We were having a new air conditioning unit put into our home, and the installer called to tell me that he was very sorry, but there was a bit of an accident. A member of the crew slipped off of a platform and put his foot through our ceiling, creating a rather large hole. He was embarrassed but unharmed. The owner was very apologetic and would make arrangements to have this properly repaired in a timely manner. A bit of an annoyance, but honestly, I was too busy to spend much time worrying about it.

As I was finishing my day, my partner came into my office and asked that I see a teen with lymphadenitis, a patient of mine but on her schedule as she was the "late" doc. My partner really did not need medical support as it was a straightforward case, but the patient was very upset with the diagnosis and was disproportionately emotional and frightened. "Apparently she lost her mother three months ago to pancreatic cancer, eight weeks after her diagnosis" my partner revealed. I looked at the name of the patient, and my heart sank. I had cared for this family for the past 15 years and knew them well. Her mom must have been in her forties, an artistic and animated lady, an architect. They were always a pleasure to see for their annual well visits. This teen was in my office a year ago, has morbid obesity and some associated depression, and I remember feeling very worried about her weight and emotions at that time. We got her into mental health and nutritional services; I reached out to her a month later and left a message on her cell phone, then never heard back from them until that day.

I felt disbelief and sorrow as I entered the room and hugged this sobbing teen. I could help reassure her that there was nothing to fear about her own health due to her lymphadenitis, tell her that it was a minor and easily treated condition, and that all illness does not result in tragedy. What could I possibly say to her about her mom? That I always really enjoyed her, or that the girl would eventually adjust? Ask her if she was in counseling and that I was there to help support her? It all seemed so trivial, and upon leaving the room I felt let down that my role as physician healer in this situation was quite limited. I noticed she had gained more weight and that, coupled with her depression around the loss of her mother, seemed insurmountable. The intervention necessary to help this teen lose weight, deal with her underlying depression, especially in the setting of such extraordinary grief, overwhelmed me.

I came home much later that night feeling emotionally exhausted. As I walked up my stairs, I saw the large gaping hole in my ceiling. Trivial, I thought, in comparison to the hole in this young teenager's heart. The inconvenience of my domestic problem of the day was just that, an inconvenience. Not a tragedy. Life is filled with both, and there is nothing more impactful about a day practicing medicine to put it all into perspective.

◆

diagram the heart

MEHA SEMWAL

i dare you: find the arteries & trace the flow of blood, the branching & exactness
with which we can be & unsee: the abdominal aorta is enormous, two fingers wide,
we marvel at its creation & how we know if our bodies had children: the women

will have enlarged ovarian vessels, their babies hungry for blood & milk & attention
so much so their mother's body changes & remains changed until she passes away
from coronary failure at sixty six, donates her body to silence—

i'm sorry I meant science—i'm not of this bitter ilk, to be unaffected at the thought
of vessels siphoning us away until we're nothing but ossified sternoclavicular
ligaments, & dissected joints so four boy-men can peer into cavities, probe canals,
remove lungs &

deign them healthy or not, the fat too much or not, & how they take the bone saw
& leave it out for us to clean, just like the dishes, like the wars, like all the
bluefin tuna that aren't there anymore: messes, cancerous masses, for someone else,
not this wide-eyed charming

exerting the gravitational force of the cocky, the uncolored, the unwomen, the
unpoor, the whom-test-questions-are-written-for: all the while tricking us into
thinking they're our answer & we're just what our bodies do: vessels enlarging for
children & men

◆

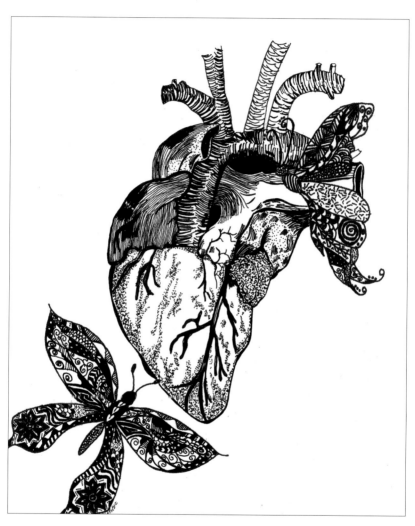

heART flutters

MCKENZIE WINTER

Joan's Smile

STACEY WYNNE-URBANOWICZ

She stands just above 5 feet and 2 inches strong in front
of eager minds with a disarming smile.
A smile that communicates so much:
"I have faith in you."
"You're close, keep trying."
"I see where you are going, but no."
"I have no idea what you are asking me, but I have faith that you
will be able to communicate it if I just keep listening and smiling."
"No, you are not an idiot, and you don't have all the answers,
that is why I'm here for you."

Most of all it says,
"I love my job."

◆

Hangin' Out

MICHELLE ALLETAG

Ginza Nights

HUY PHAN

Kauai sunset

PATRICIA NASH

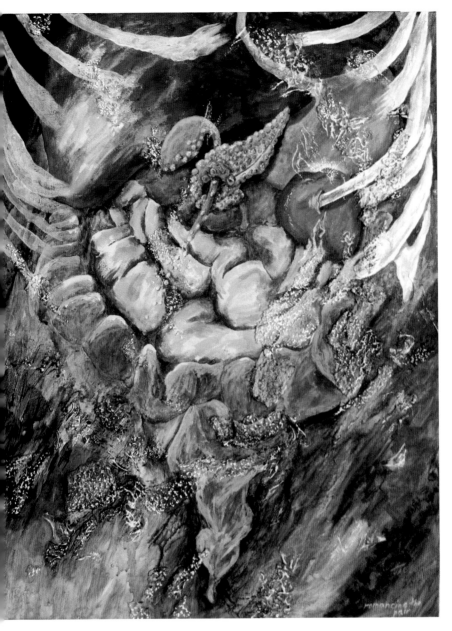

romancing the pain

THE POET SPIEL

Don't ever be an interesting patient

ALEXANDER GHINCEA

Don't ever be an interesting patient.

We come in droves: students, residents, attendings. We come to see your disease, to touch, to feel, to hear. We come to learn. We pontificate on rounds, scratch our chins, offer next steps. We invite teams of specialists to solicit their expert opinions. We spend hour after hour agonizing over your lab results and your scans, searching for clues. We stay up late reading case reports, straining for an answer.

Don't ever be an interesting patient, lest *you* get lost in the complexity of your disease.

You're 40 years old, and you will never work again. You may not even be able to walk. If you make it out of the hospital, it will be to a nursing home. To you, we are a never-ending parade of white coats and stethoscopes. You can't see behind the scenes. Those labs and scans matter very little… except that they involve another needle, another hour in a claustrophobic box. A soft touch, a few quiet moments spent in silence. These are what you value most.

Please understand that to us, you're an interesting patient.

We have no explanation for your disease, and certainly no semblance of a cure. It's agonizing to see you in pain, to see you emaciated and sick. We are powerless spectators in the face of your disease, and sometimes we forget that *you* are still there, suffering. When we do, please call us back. Remind us that *you* are the reason we went into medicine, not your disease. Remind us that you're not just an interesting patient.

◆

Zusha

SIMON M. KAMAU

*Zusha [Speak up] campaign makes a clarion call
on Kenyans to: 'Speak up, Silence is killing us!
Do not let a reckless driver make you end up like this!'
Tis' an effort in the right direction–
Urges passengers to speak against reckless
driving on location.
It targets effecting behaviour change;
making safety a personal responsibility.*

*But then are they not the same Kenyans who in some
parts of this country rebuke others who dare speak;
look you curiously for fidgeting with the safety belt?
Or 'carefully observe' that the complaining passenger -
must be a new one to the route.*

*The average Kenyan passenger is a double standards -
It depends person.
In some trips he is heard to say–once the matatu
(a taxi van) is full
(and by this he means–one passenger per seat), 'let's go!'
In other circumstances he is a passive one that will
ease up that same space so that many more can come
in;
including helping create illegal makeshift link
'sambaza-seats' in all available aisle and leg spaces.*

One day a desperate sojourner burst out reminding
fellow passengers; even as they overload, there
would be no gauze bandages or gloves in the hospital–
Should there be any injuries.
From the confines, another passenger pronounced;
in no uncertain terms that–everyone involved would not be–
Be what!?
Be eligible to any insurance compensation should they get involved
in an accident.
They glared at the 12x3 inch Zusha stickers,
a few shook their heads. Someone muttered, 'sasa hii ni nini?'
(Swahili for–what's this now?).
No one could dare: 'Speak up!'
A sicker sticker portrayed a dead body on a stretcher;
another sticky one had resisted attempts to scrape it,
showed an incongruous mangled wreck
of a look-alike matatu. Same Sacco–
How comes?

The blast–No not the blast, the bang; whichever!
The silence that followed was deafening.
Zusha–doing nothing is not an option;
me I'll Zusha,
Be the passenger in the driver's seat,
even if it's not more noble -
Haply Be safe

◆

This piece is a reflection on the Zusha Road Safety
Campaign in Kenya (www.zusharoadsafety.org).
Between 3000 and 13,000 Kenyans lose their lives
in traffic-related collisions every year.

Push

MATTHEW WOOD

1…. Phone rings. How is it that my ringtone, which I love at 3 pm, is so piercing at 3 am? Get up. Missing sleep. Tired and unable to focus. Drive across town. Not a single car occupies the road with me.

2…. Badge into the back entrance of the hospital. I'm still amazed they let me do this. I get to work in the hospital. I've dreamed of this for years and somehow they actually let me do it. I still feel like it's a mistake and someone is going to rectify their error.

3…. Scrubs. Still creased from sitting folded for so long. The same soft blue as every other hospital. A fleeting thought: it's interesting that we wear disposable clothes because blood is such a daily part of our lives.

4…. My attending is here. I've never made it in before him. No matter how many lights I accidently run in my half-asleep dash across town. Maybe he lives here. I bet his wife wouldn't like that.

5…. Mom's been in labor for hours and she's finally fully dilated. I walk in. I'm complaining about being woken up after 3 hours of sleep. She's been working since the start of my shift yesterday. Active labor has a way of preventing a mother from getting any rest.

6…. "Go ahead." Maybe it's the fact that I'm punch-drunk, but I thought my attending just told me to deliver this baby. That can't be the case. I look at his eyes, as I hesitate, not moving. He nods at our patient, almost imperceptible. He actually meant it. My heart goes from 60 to 160 before I take the two steps that place me at the end of our soon-to-be-mother's bed. I've seen this done before. Right? I can't remember if that's actually true. I feel like it should be, but no recollection comes to mind.

7…. "Mas, mas, mas, mas, mas!" Spanish speaking only. The first baby that I get to deliver and I can't communicate with the mother. No other words from high school Spanish come back to mind. Hola? Biblioteca? Estudiante? Mas? More? "More, more, more!" It's all I've got.

8…. Keep pushing, Momma. She looks so exhausted. Sweat pouring down her face. She's been pushing for 3 hours now. She probably stopped believing us that she's making progress. We have her husband ask if she wants to feel her baby's head. She cries. One
of the most beautiful things I've ever seen. Her next push is that best one yet.

9…. Baby. I go through the motions that my mind has cobbled together. Support the head. Anterior shoulder first. Posterior second. It still astounds me how blue they are when their first born. It is the longest, most-agonizing 10 seconds of my life waiting for a sound. The first cry shatters the silence and I take my first breath in time. Dad cuts the cord. Mom cradles baby. Proud parents. So worth it.

10…. Deep breath.

◆

Happening upon an Eastern fence lizard hatchling
(Sceloporus undulates)

REBECCA HOLLMANN

The Land of Limbo

JEAN ABBOTT

She was feisty and independent and had soldiered into old age like many of her generation–actually coming to relish the retirement community imposed upon her when her husband died and the 2-story colonial became too much. A busy phone life talking to friends and relatives, comparing our Denver weather with that in Georgia, highlighting her TV guide in pink for her favorite game shows and the sports teams she followed, and always ready for her carefully-timed meals with the 3 Bettys–her pals with their fleet of walkers.

I guess a stroke was among the predictable ways that this chapter could have ended. One of those life-changing little clots, floating out of her fibrillating atrium into her left MCA. Found by a friend when she didn't pick up her paper–these widows watched out for each other. There was the call from the ER, the days of testing, the 3 weeks of rehab, the move to Colorado. A disorienting blur for us–what was it for her? While the right-sided weakness resolved into mere neglect, the aphasia remained. There were a couple of recognizable times when she said: "I wish I could shoot myself." But for the most part: word salad, garbled sentences, sometimes insistent paragraphs (often complete with finger wagging) that defied our ability to interpret. There were sighs, some tears, a few "Oh, jeez!"–but more remarkable were the chuckling, quirky facial expressions and the good-humored acceptance of her situation. It felt to us like the not-quite-big-enough stroke. But was that my own voice speaking?

This descent from independence had a silver lining for us, at least. We heard stories from her friends. My crusty, often-complaining mother-in-law turns out to have been the good-natured leader of her retirement home "family." The one who wouldn't let people gossip, the one who learned the names of all the 300 residents over her 5 years there. Beloved by her friends who allowed us to see her in a new light.

Then, as so often happens, came the next blow in her frail trajectory. Nighttime confusion, a fall that broke a bone in her hand. Not painful and not something she would keep even a tiny protective splint on–as ugly as it looked to her doctor kids on her Xray. The next fall–this was the big one, though perhaps not big enough. By now she was on a fancy new blood thinner. Multiple rib fractures, pneumothorax, hemothorax; a small catheter, followed by a bigger one. More confusion, delirium, hallucinations, unable to rest, wincing with pain. Unable to feed herself, needing to be turned. A rare intelligible response: "Do you want another bite of mashed potatoes?" "No, I want to die." The messy family discussions about how far to go– so much more complicated than all the talks I have given and sanitized narratives I have heard from others of descents towards death. What does "comfort care" look like? What is too invasive? We had talked about what we might do if she fell and broke her hip. A flail chest turns out to be a lot worse–no quick fix, no quick death.

I sat at her bedside tonight–she has regained her garbled word salad, some awareness, endearing smiles and childlike waves at all who care for her. It's been 10 days since her fall, and she is better. She will soon go back to her apartment with major support from a swarm of caregivers. But as I approached her bed tonight, she was curled up like a child, sobbing. We held hands, saying little. Her pain is one I don't know how to respond to: "I'm lonely." She is so sad, so tired of living.

My mother's parents died quickly. In my lifetime, those quick deaths have become rare. I have devoted my working life to that triad of cure, comfort, and caring. People like mom live longer and adapt their lives to their multiple maladies. The exit will come–soon or not so soon. But she's reached that point in the arc of her life when death is a gift, a blessed relief from the fight. Her life was well-enough lived–that oh-so-human messy mix of joy and regret. And meanwhile we wait with her. Suspended in the space that is not quite living and not quite death.

◆

The Death of My Patient Last Week

L. A. KAHN

Eight days ago, my patient died. His name escapes me, though I used it many times in the hours that I knew him; its recollection is lost in the wash of biological details I collected and faithfully catalogued. The human spirit may exist beyond the material plane, but the mundane markers of daily wear are what we see and respond to. Like concentration camp prisoners stripped of clothes and hair, bereft of the symbols of the lives they had, there is an irrevocable loss of personality that occurs upon hospitalization. Patients replace their chosen clothing with hospital gowns and skidproof socks, carry machines in their flesh tethering them to information networks, require assistance in removing waste from their orifices. They merge into an undifferentiated mass of needs, one beast calling out from many beds, a smudge of human suffering distinguished only by the order in which their systems break down. I don't remember my patient's name because it was irrelevant; I instead remember the course of events that took him, the shocking CT scan, the failed surgical attempt, the pressors and traumas of the last hours. The detail of my documentation was in his death, not his life.

*   *   *

On hospital days, the dichotomy becomes unbearable: five physicians in a ward room, dressed exhaustively in professional gear, shoes shined, ties and badges abreast and clipboards in hand. We stand around the bed of the patient below us–barefoot, pasty, un-garbed. We talk to each other about the patient, in front of the patient, a convention unacceptable in the bright world outside. We tell each other how much salt is in their blood, how much blood is in their urine, how much urine they have produced in the past twenty-four hours. We speak in code about their perceived motives and desires. We tell each other what we think we should do, confirm and veto plans, roll the patient back and forth to hear various organs, examine tubes carefully. We make mental lists of things to do as we answer their questions, and rub antiseptic gel on our hands as we walk briskly out of the room to the next failing creature.

*   *   *

My patient who died eight days ago was a freshwater biologist before he retired. He and his wife enjoyed going to concerts and eating out around town. He died the night I admitted him, suddenly, unexpectedly, amidst much rancor between medical teams. There was blame to spare the next morning. I scrolled through his CT scans again and again, searching for a sign we'd missed on admission, a predictor of what the next twelve hours would bring. I didn't see his body or his family; they were inaccessible, buried in the ICU behind a cluster of professionals. I wanted to see his wife –to do what? Cry with her? Apologize for laughing so casually the night before? Share my bewilderment, as though it could provide solace?

My patient's CT scan from admission stays with me: the black and gray images of his colon, the hunt for signs of inflammation, the contested slide that might have showed dead tissue. I remember, too, his physical exam from the night before, his abdomen distended but not taut, tender to the touch in only a few places, his lungs clear, his ankles a little swollen. His feet were sensitive, from some longstanding nerve damage. I remember how much oxygen he needed and that his potassium was normal. I do not remember his name.

◆

From: Animal Stories

JENNIE HAMMET

It's easier to imagine animals living like people than people living like animals. After all, in the animal world, whoever's bigger always seems to win. People would never dream of living that way.

Bill goes hunting all the time. He has a stuffed pheasant in his house. When he moved, the movers kept calling it a peacock. "Where do you want the peacock?" they'd ask.

He said he could never shoot a deer, because of their big, melting eyes. I'll bet the quail and pheasants are bitter, being made with little, beady eyes.

There are five wishbones on the sill of his kitchen window.

Instead of training birds simply to talk, I think we should train them to run talk shows, then gradually to run entire radio stations.

My friends were telling me at dinner of their drive. A bird hopped into the road unexpectedly, and Jim hit him with the right front tire and kept going. Parts of the bird stuck to the tire and kept going 'round: whump, whump, whump. Suddenly, the chicken salad wasn't as enjoyable.

When people are camping, they often put their food in trees so as not to attract bears. This technique never helped the bees.

When I was little, my father caught a catfish. He was fishing for trout, and no one ended up cleaning it. Catfish are so bony. It sat in the sink until someone finally threw it away. I still feel bad about that fish.

My friend Vicki talks to animals all the time. If you're eating with her outdoors, she'll tell the flies to go away; but she'll do it in a very gentle way, as if they were her children. If she isn't eating and trying to keep them from landing on her food, she'll watch them closely to learn more about their lifestyle.

Garth said someone in his building kept a rabbit in a shopping cart and never let it out. He was going to call the animal shelter to possibly rescue it, but I'm sure he didn't. I wonder if that ever bothers him.

When Jonathan moved out of his place on Cole Street, the last thing we took over to his new house was Hazel, his goldfish. We were all on our way somewhere, and he was going to go up and put her in the bathtub so she could go for a swim while he was away. He turned on the hot water, though, and killed her. He just wasn't thinking.

Animals don't usually try to alter their moods. They also never take acting class, and few of them ever eat in Chinese restaurants, though Mexican is popular. More filling.

Is it true that the more desirable an animal is to predators, the hornier it is? This would make sense.

The coyotes will still be living in L.A. long after the people expire. Again, Mexican food. One of the reasons they would continue to survive is their paws won't work in such a way as to enable them to open SPAM cans.

Why do dogs howl at the moon? Is it that the moon seems to be evading them? Dogs can't stand that. My father says he used to get the coyotes to howl at night by howling. So maybe dogs aren't howling at the moon. Maybe some kid is making them do it.

In the summer, the bats fly out of Carlsbad Caverns every evening and back again at dawn. It is said they go to Mexico to feed. Again, Mexican food.
Q: How do they know when it's time to leave, if it's dark there in the caves, anyway?
A: They get hungry. They smell tortillas. They go.

Some people get upset when people give animals human characteristics. But animals do the same thing to humans. Just look at an animal who thinks you're going to steal its food, when it's dog food. Just think about that.

In fact, people go into hibernation, too—sometimes for generations.

Herons are often seen standing in the middle of a swamp, waiting for fish to happen. When he catches a fish, a heron must toss it up in the air and catch it so it goes down his throat head first; for he swallows the fish whole—and if it got stuck sideways, his mother would keep calling and calling and calling, but she would never, ever again get an answer.

Dogs eat shit sometimes. I don't know why they do that.

If a bird ate a rare flower, this would make the bird rare, too.

A professor of classics I know shows slides of undersea life during the first meeting of his mythology class each term, "…because," he says, "If you know something like this really exists on earth, you'll know that anything is possible."

___

continued on next page…

Two poems

Strange sound

Every time you hear a strange sound,
               You jump.
You never leave your ears to flop lazily around.
   They're always busy.
Let this be a cue to our meeting someplace quiet,
   Desolate as silent thunder.

Lion
If you were a lion I'd put my head in your mouth
Just to show I trusted you
I would feel your hot breath on my scalp
The jagged toothy edge against my neck like an unzipped zipper.
You could not see me squeeze my frightened eyes tight when I have my head there,
How could you?

Poodles in the microwave, kittens in the dryer. I see a cement truck outside, and I don't even want to think about it.

My sister doesn't think animal rights activists should wear leather shoes.

Ralf remembers years ago gathering starfish at the North Sea and taking them back to boil them at his friend's tiny flat, making the whole place stink terribly. He thought it was funny, especially because he had a bigger, sweeter-smelling place to go home to.

Martha doesn't eat meat and talks about dead animals when she mentions it, and so I tried the shoe leather logic on her, but she said, "There are various reasons for not eating meat." Well, I knew that. I guess she just doesn't like meat, or her father force-fed her meat when she was a child, or she was conserving food. But when it comes down to dead animals, she WAS wearing them on her feet.

Mark used to be pretty content with a mostly vegetarian diet until he found out in his Cultural Anthropology class that one of the great steps in the evolution of man was when man began to eat meat. The eating of animal flesh was supposed to have expanded man's cranial capacity. All of a sudden, Mark wanted to eat meat. More meat! T-bone! Chicken! Pork chop! So what if all of this evolution didn't happen in one lifetime, and it was too late for HIS cranial capacity? Or maybe it wasn't the meat itself--maybe people simply became smarter because the not-so-smart hunters starved to death? He's smart enough already, anyway. But this sure makes a good story.

Animals want all the food for themselves. People would never do that.

Did the big dinosaurs pick on the little dinosaurs?
Did the little dinosaurs laugh and run between the big dinosaurs' legs?

Cats can tell if you are sincere or not when you are petting them. I believe cats know immediately, without looking, who is touching them. Even if they're asleep, they know.

I used to think a pointer dog pointed with his tail. I used to look at dog breeds in the World Book Encyclopedia, and the pointer had his tail straight out. In fact, I am still half convinced he points with his tail.

I don't think Lassie really did half those things.

The male crickets sing, the male canaries sing, and the female mosquitoes bite. Don't keep those females too hungry.

Did the cows at the birth of Jesus care very much about the whole thing?
Did the ox and lamb really keep time?

I remember bugs that looked like sticks and bugs that looked like leaves. This they have as a very sophisticated camouflage. What worries me is there could be bug that looks like your mother or your priest.

There are some animals who don't trust anybody. Usually, nothing happens to them.

◆

Paul

JENNIE HAMMETT

Paul used to be a boxer
he was small and quick and mean
he'd come in with a jab to your cheekbone
Ice it down.

What else was there for a poor Irish kid to do but box? he asks me
Well, Paul, not sit around and dream they were Kennedys
even if they do drive drunk

I wonder about him, so young & small
learning to take a punch to the jaw
And he'd release his neck and look up at the stars—the physics of the punch

He learned to keep his chin down
Paul made a name, free of residue
Kids in accordance with an acre and a half
of bleating white sheep

◆

Close Call

DAVID WEIL

Buddha killed the Betta

MICHELLE COLARELLI

My son was seven when we lost our 18-year-old cat. She had the sweetest of souls. She was so gentle that she interacted with my son only when he was calm, quiet, and cuddly. She loved to curl between our legs as we slept and would often be found in my lap or tucked far from his reach under the bed. He loved her dearly but secretly hoped for a new, more playful pet.

When he realized that we would not be getting a dog he started begging for a guinea pig, hamster, turtle, or a snake… I quickly agreed to a fish and thwarted any more conversations of reptiles.

We journeyed to the local pet store, and I told the clerk we wanted something very simple. It would be the first time I ever cared for a fish. She guided us through the purchase of a 2-gallon fish bowl and a Betta. In choosing the decorations I presumed we would be going for a pirate theme and held out a treasure chest, but my son shook his head "no" and held up a Buddha.

My heart melted. We found a pink lotus flower, a sponge ball of a plant to collect his waste, and some pearl colored shale. I was certainly content. Next my son chose the fish, and off we went. As we stood in line to pay, he announced to anyone that would listen, "We are naming our fish Fred!"

Call it a premonition if you wish, but my first thought was, oh honey, I hope I don't ever have to tell you, "Fred's dead, baby. Fred's dead." I pushed the thought aside and tried to laugh off my mind's reference to a scene in Pulp Fiction.

At home, I was so pleased with the set up. The fish bowl was a perfect addition to my son's dresser, especially with the backdrop of a large picture we had of a rocky shoreline and sandy beach. Fred swam towards it as though he was going home. Imagine a life size view of the ocean. He loved it.

Fred was a cool cat of a fish, just as chill as our cat. I bragged about him loving Reiki in my yoga class. Everyone laughed. "How do you know what a fish feels?" they asked. I did not know how to explain how I knew; I could just feel it. He also loved to dance. I swear! I danced with him daily. He was my little Fred Astaire.

On that first weekend my son was with his father, and he checked in with me so often it made me laugh. "Did you feed Freddy?" he would text. "Could you send us a picture?" I assured him that I absolutely loved Fred and was caring for him dearly.

I made a ritual of cleaning the tank that first Sunday. It would coincide with caring for my plants. I looked to it like a prayer, or a weekly meditation. I joyfully scrubbed the bowl and buffed the Buddha, as I would care for a client: gentle, soothing, and mindful.

Yet, I got sloppy in the end.

The directions said not to replace all the water in the bowl. So I didn't. I was to replace only one half to one third. So I did. Yet, after cleaning the Buddha, he became more of a weeble wobble than an astute statue when I tried to replace him in the tank.

I knew it wasn't right. If I was truly being mindful, I would have adhered to the daily living mantra, "everything has a place, and everything is in its place." Right? This statue certainly was not in his place, hovering slightly above the surface on any given side. Yet, I chose to walk away and left him for the night.

The next day my son returned home and ran immediately to feed Fred. "He's DEAD!" he screamed from his room. My heart shattered. "What?!?!?"

"He's DEAD!!! You killed him!"

No, no, no, no, no! I thought running to the bowl. But there he was pinned by the Buddha. At first I was in denial. ~ I could not have killed Fred. ~ I loved Fred. ~ He was my buddy…

Buddha killed the Betta.

◆

The Words Unspoken

L. A. KAHN

The baby's mom was young and pretty, with big brown eyes and a long braid down her back. She was devoted to her son. I saw her every day of my service, and, as far as I could tell, she never left the hospital. She soothed him as he fussed, adjusted the feeding tube taped to his cheek, sang to him as he lay responseless. She thought she saw him blink one time, but generally seemed to accept that not much would change: that he would never nurse again, never babble, never walk; that the most she could hope for was response to light or touch; that any dreams for him had been severed the day they'd arrived.

I knew nothing of her life outside the hospital, beyond the vague impression that she'd been in school for something. She never expressed despair or showed anger toward her ex-boyfriend, who had shaken her son's head back and forth. The ex never came to the hospital. As far as I saw, she never had any visitors; it was just she and her son, still a beautiful baby with his mom's big eyes, in their quiet sunny room. As we neared his discharge date, any anger I'd had was replaced by sadness for this woman who seemed so alone, with her futureless child. Time would move forward, but he would stay suspended, in stasis, under his mom's gaze.

◆

To You

RYAN GOFFREDI

This image is a scanning electron micrograph of salt granules placed one-by-one using forceps and a dissecting microscope.

The Universe

FREDRICK ABRAMS

On a galaxy that's whirling
On its swift and endless run
There's a planet spinning madly
'Round its slowly dying sun

On the planet there are oceans
And some land that's poking through
On the land there is a river
Flowing downward, as they do

Near the river there's a farmyard
With an irrigation ditch
And a puddle drying slowly
Since the farmer pulled the switch

On the edges of the puddle
There's a fringe of greenish slime
And some bugs were gathered 'round it
At this point in boundless time

They had gathered in the puddle
When they tired of buggy play
Since their lives were spent entirely
In this quickly passing day

There was vigorous debating
With much ranting, raving strife
For they all had raised the question
Of the meaning of their life

And one simple bug had shouted
"I can see no mystery
Only God could have created
Something wonderful as me"

"For aren't we the highest
And most complex form of thing
Our puddle is the universe
Come let His praises ring"

As they bent their heads together
In a smugly prideful bow
Their universe with all of them
Was stepped on by a cow

◆

The Sudden End of the Firefight

ART ELSER

The jet races low over the fields toward the tree line
where a small cloud of white smoke rises
from a marking rocket. As the jet nears the smoke,
six shiny cans of napalm tumble from it,
two by two by two,
exploding into a rolling ball of fire
that engulfs the trees.

When the burning slows, troops move forward
to rout the enemy who has wounded
and killed their comrades.
They find only death from the fire.
Forty-five enemy killed.
There is ecstasy over the victory.

In the decades since, in nightmares,
daymares, memories, that jet races
again and again and again
to the trees and releases its napalm,
two by two by two.
But now there is no ecstasy,
only sadness and grief and guilt.

◆

Peeking in on the Downy Woodpecker (Picoides pubescens)

REBECCA HOLLMANN

Art for Healing

STEVEN LEWIS

If I Was Good to You

CHRISTINE MITCHELL

This unique submission is an original song written, sung, and performed on guitar by Christine Mitchell with her former band, "droplet". Droplet was a 3 piece band with Greg Lyon on bass, Troy Berg on Drums, and Christine Mitchell on vocals and guitar. This song was independently recorded without affiliation to a record label.

The audio recording may be listened to at the following web address: http://www.ucdenver.edu/thehumantouch

Daffodil

ANJALI DHURANDHAR

Spouting Rock Waterfall

DAVID ECKHARDT

Untitled

ELIZABETH SWIFT

Where have you been?
Right here.
Why have you gone?
I haven't.
How can I find you?
Be still.

◆

Diá del Juego

JAMES ENGELN

The roosters signal the arrival of daybreak, and the asses echo their alarm. The air is fresh and clean. A morning mist clings to the vegetation in the fields, still waiting for the first rays of the sun. Scattered chimneys throw up the white smoke of breakfast and coffee, but the majority of the houses of El Bosque are still quiet. No one sets out to tend the fields today, and there are no *motos* carrying people to town. The cheerful din of children preparing for school is absent, and there is no sound of banter or bargaining at the *colmado*. The *campo* is slow to rise this morning.

Morning is a special time in the Caribbean. It presents incredible opportunity and the promise of another day to accomplish what was squandered or abandoned in yesterday's scorching heat. People are fresh and animated, not yet worn down by toil and baking temperatures. Even the colors of the landscape benefit from night's reprieve from the glaring equatorial sun. Everything is alive and willing and full of hope.

Unique to this morning is a vim and vigor in excess of any other. This energy was allowed to grow in the slowness of the dawn and now exudes from every corner of the *campo*. It excites the children and finally draws them out of their homes. They congregate in boisterous groups, each one brandishing a tattered glove or tired bat. A ball regularly ejects from the middle of the children, and every eligible pair of hands scrambles to make the catch. They are headed to the baseball diamond for their turn at bat.

Women are next to emerge from the clusters of split palm houses with rusted tin roofs. Not yet dressed in their Sunday finest, their hair still in rollers, they stroll from neighbor to neighbor in route to the *colmado* for a few final ingredients for the midday meal. They gossip and flirt, adding to this morning's vitality.

Finally, the bright white pinstripe pants and brilliant red jerseys of Los Tigres del Bosque step out into the morning that has built in their anticipation. The uniforms may well be the cleanest, most well kept clothing these men own. It is in direct contrast to their *vestido del compasino*, worn and faded by the demands of life in this rural, *batey* community. Today, second hand shirts are replaced by pinstripes, *la lucha* is exchanged for competition. Today is *el diá del juego*, game day, in El Bosque, Dominican Republic.

Excitement continues to build throughout the morning, but the sun climbs higher and intensifies its efforts to defeat the ambition of those foolish enough to test its will. Sweaty young children return from the *play*, exhausted by their gaming and the climbing temperature. The heat and humidity cannot kill the spirit today; because today there will be an opportunity for escape.

The red jerseys of Los Tigres have departed from the shady recesses where they had gathered to begin their game day preparations. Baseball fans in all forms of friends, family, and neighbors come together in groups and start to move in the direction of the field. They move along slowly from house to house, saying hello, drinking coffee, and making the appropriate inquiries of life and family. In this way, the crowd grows in numbers and "rushes" to the field. In truth, if they arrive before the first pitch it will be an anomaly.

The *play*, Dominican for baseball field, has the idyllic feel of Sunday afternoon at the ballpark. Clusters of spectators are scattered around the diamond, leaning against their *motos*, or tending a sweaty mare. Youth flit from here to there, chasing each other and stray balls. Players are spread across the field, warming up with major-league commitment and concentration. The umpire, dressed in stripes, circles the bases to ensure proper placement and spacing. It is a scene to rival any major league ballpark.

The *play* is literally carved out of the jungle. In place of the outfield wall is an arc of ceiba and almond trees. Two lone palms stand as foul posts. It is El Bosque's version of Fenway's Green Giant. A home run is awarded for baseballs that reach the jungle on the fly; a ground rule double is granted for any other that escapes the field of play on the hop. All fly balls are at the mercy of the underbrush and may never return to active duty.

The grass is closely cropped by the herd of horses that makes pasture on the *play* during the week. Their manure fertilizes the field while their appetites ensure a level surface. Last night, the "grounds crew" was moved to another pasture and the larger mounds of fertilizer were removed.

This morning, after the kids had their turn on the mound, the diamond was raked by hand. Horse blankets were laid out as makeshift bases and the foul lines were painted in by the umpire. Completing the *play* is a cement and chain link backstop. Its cinderblocks are riddled with holes from wild pitches and errant fast-balls.

The fans are really arriving now and are ready to make their presence known. They fill in the shade under makeshift canopies and pile on the rocks down the third base line. People squint in the sun, sweat, and cheer. Wherever the vantage point, whatever the conditions, no would want to miss their Tigres take on their rivals from El Dean.

After a brief meeting between the umpire and the team managers, it is time to play ball! Los Tigres del Bosque take the field. The red jerseys jog out to their positions and the visiting players of El Dean retreat to scraps of shade along the first base line, their "dugout". The pitcher takes the mound. The crowd cheers for the local heater as he eyes his first pitch. He unwinds and releases the ball, sending it streaking to home plate. Strike one!

continued on next page…

The game is on. Bats fly and gloves flash and the crowd is loving every minute of it. They cheer for ground balls, strikeouts, fly-outs, and double plays. The players are invigorated by the support, confirming their drive to win.

A questionable call from the umpire and tempers flare. Managers march out of shady dugouts to contest the call. They meet head-on to present their views. Every opinion is emphasized in spit, every argument reinforced with physical language. This is the Sunday game, and nothing is to be taken lightly.

This is no Wriggly Field, and these are certainly not the New York Yankees, but they play as if it was and as if they were. They are not discouraged because they have to share equipment and exchange gloves with their rivals every half inning. No one is above searching the underbrush for a home run ball, and no one is beneath posing at the plate to emphasize the hit that reaches the jungle on the fly. This is pure, unadulterated Dominican baseball. It is dramatic and beautiful.

Los Tigres step up to the plate to begin the ninth inning. Down five runs to El Dean they are in desperate need of a magnificent rally. CRACK, base hit. CRACK, ground rule double. CRACK, base hit. The offense is alive, and the comeback is on! The good guys are only down one, and the winning run is on second. Next to the plate is Los Tigres' best slugger. No one wants to miss out on the thrill of victory, and the crowd is wild with anticipation.

Drenched in sweat, his pinstripe pants stained a rusty red, the last chance for Los Tigres del Bosque digs in at home plate. On the mound, the pitcher from El Dean knows he only needs this out to silence the crowd and send them home in bitter defeat. Strike one. Strike two. This is it…

CRACK. Home run! The batter knows it, the crowd knows it, and the pitcher hangs his head because he knows it too. All of the spirit and hope that buoyed the morning is realized in this moment. Red jerseys mob their hero as he jumps onto home plate. Celebrations erupt from the crowd. Men, women and children alike run and jump with joy. Such great release, such simple circumstance.

It is late afternoon now, and the players have long since abandoned the *play*. Today, the character of the people and the strength of the community were victorious. They were champions over the reality of their circumstance and the oppressive truths of poverty. The conditions of life for these marginalized populations that undermine the psyche and crush the ambition of the individual; they did not defeat the people today. For a moment, it was ok to celebrate, it was ok to dream. Tomorrow, when the withering Caribbean sun returns, the game will begin again. But tomorrow there will be no baseball.

◆

Keep Climbing

NASSER ALSALEH

It's All in Her Head

CAROL CALKINS

Didn't feel quite right
Suddenly sensitive to noise and light
Headaches and pain
Body and mind felt drained

Had a bunch of tests
Needed to rest
Things got worse
It's all in her head

Went from place to place
Find someone who knew
But it seems so real
No, it's all in her head

Can't even walk
Eat one meal a day
Trapped in quiet and dark
It's all in her head?

Finally it's confirmed
Advanced Lyme Disease
Throughout body and brain
Others still think it's all in her head

Has affected her cells
Organ function not well
Illness taking over
NOW it is in her head!

Unable to move
Family cares and comforts her
Fly across the country
For the one who believes

Sad such a young person
Is so extremely ill
Pray she recovers
Hope it's not too late

Although things are bad
Bond with others who care
Keeps them all going
Despite the fear

Family have faith
With true belief
Healing will take place
Soon she'll be safe

◆

Bangkok

OREN M GORDON

Manliness is an epidemic
that made its way to Thailand and
found fertility as the apex illness
in the spicy food and the swagger of the ladyboys
accentuating lithe muscles, bony shins and phallic knuckles
sleeping under tattoos and burn scars;

Muay Thai fights are not so popular anywhere but Thailand
in that smiling country a man, is a fighter
and the farang that pour into the country speak too bluntly
with money, but no strength
to take a hot pepper
or a single kick.

Fighting is no hobby here
gyms, temples, and beaches spoon under sweaty stars
whispering sweet nothings to the sea
while men lying in the streets,
all say the same words
that they rumble in every ear walking by
though most are far too busy
with the spicy food
or the swagger of a ladyboy.

◆

Bones

RACHAEL RUFF

They start so soft and vulnerable.
Can poke them with a pencil, spear what they protect inside.

But soon they grow and harden.
They speak of the grace and power to come.

At the peak they are invincible.
An impenetrable force that evokes immortality.

It does not last.

They become weak. Become filled with useless air contained by a thinning sheath.
They betray with a snap where they once would only bend.

The story of their life is told through marks more permanent than tattoos.
And they remain long after the rest has gone, waiting for the embrace of the Earth.

◆

on depression

SALLY PEACH

and then,

      darkness.

As if the page turn
landed in purgatory:
Wilting midnight claws
dredging through
and on and on

       and

On a Monday,
you pretend.
On a Tuesday,
you pretend.
we must be careful
who we pretend to be
On a Wednesday,

       you pretend

that there is no
gnawing from the shadows
and horseplay after dark
nor sickles aired in silence
or absentia in the heart

the little girl's dress-up gown
is black lace and lamé
(but it is all just a game of)

pretend
and then,

◆

Art for Healing

STEVEN LEWIS

Relaxing landscapes

JAMES GEYMAN

Great Blue Heron chasing away nest robbing cormorant

GEORGE HO, JR.

Workin' The Catapult

MICHAEL AUBREY

Two Pediatrics Stories in 55 Words

EMILY HAUSE

Breathe in. Breathe out.
Tiny lungs working
Gasping. Struggling.
Small, frightened eyes searching for Mom's face.
Looking for comfort from behind the bars of the crib.
Clinical words to describe reality:
Increased work.
Stridor.
Belly breathing.
Retractions.
All those words sum up the awful truth- your child can't breathe.
It's that season, says my resident

Mom drank and got high while she was pregnant. She gave him up for adoption.
His small, underdeveloped body is riddled with diagnoses: anencephaly, developmental delay, gastric motility issues, precocious puberty to name just a few.
He's admitted for unrelenting seizure activity. This is his new baseline.
He's got a good heart, says his grandmother

◆

*The "Punkin Chunkin Colorado" event
is held annually in Aurora. It is truly
an odd and inspiring event: How far
can one catapult or blast a pumpkin?*

Goodbye-Hello

CLAIRE RAMIREZ

Goodbye touch

My grandpa is napping in a coffin
Appears as if at any moment he might open his eyes
Share another story about Lassie
Make me juevos con weenies
Shuffle a pack of cards with such speed
The cards melting together, a blur of motion
The sound mimicking the steady drum of his fingers
Sensing the cards through vibrating wood
Beats me at Poison once again

My grandpa is napping in a coffin
Everyone tiptoes around him
Whispers softly to one another
I reach for his hand
Cold
Not an ice cold
When you make a snowball with bare fingers
Or jump into a pool during winter
The biting water piercing so deeply you forget how to breathe
Not that cold
A cold unmoved by warmth
I place one hand underneath and one hand above
I wonder why they made my grandpa appear to be napping
I wonder if that's why people touch his hands
A reminder that he is not
A reminder to say goodbye

Hello touch

The nurse asks me if I want to hold my nephew
Before I can respond, I find him in my arms
His movements, his skin, his small mews
All so new, untouched by the world
His fingers are tiny pink twigs
I am afraid of breaking such fragility
With a whisper of my index finger, I gently stroke the creases of his palm
His fingers instantly curl around the tip of my finger
My head knows this is just a reflex
My heart tells me it is so much more
It is the birth of love

◆

A Letter to My Guru

MICHAEL HIMAWAN

I have seen it written that this world is a charnel ground.

From the moment of our birth,
We are subject to the inevitabilities of aging
And of illness, and death, and change.
All of these things I have read and heard.

But none of it made real until the moment I first saw you
Lying there, one of eight great teachers
Who came to us in Love.

And realer still at the first cut:
How easy it is for metal to rend flesh
And for the implements of human invention
To score our skin.

Questions came as like a river
Washing over a master and his disciples.
"What is this called? And that?"
"Have I found what I am looking for?"
And, "How will I know if I've gone too far?"

As you waited patiently for us to find the answers
You'd entrusted to our care.

On the day of our parting, one answer still eluded me
Even in spite of all your teachings:

What measure of gratitude could ever suffice to repay
One who gives away everything he has?

Other than to practice with the utmost diligence
Striving, always, to embody your grace.

◆

"She released a small cloud of telepathic butterflies... Oh my, oh my."*

BRIANNA SMYK

Francesca sat cross-legged on the floor, collapsed over her grandmother's antique coffee table. Tapping a yellow No. 2 with her left hand and palming her heavy head in her right, she stared out her window into the white void of a blizzard.

Glancing at her notebook, she focused on the few sentences written in her tight, boxy print. She reread the eulogy but couldn't fathom how any combination of words could sum up her mother.

Sitting up to take a sip of her hot toddy, she sighed as the liquid melted through her throbbing insides. She moved the mug to her forehead. Heat soaked into her third eye and hands, softening her arms back to the table's lacquered veneer.

Her gaze drifted across the floor, through the forest of crumpled papers to her yawning laptop, which cast a neon blue glow into the white light of the storm.

Even from across her living room, the cursor of her research grant application tapped its foot, reminding her that if she wanted to study the clear-winged *Cithaerias pireta* butterfly in the Amazon, she didn't have time to fold into a cocoon of grief.

Looking back to the window, afterimages of the screen played a geometric trick of the eye. Computer-shaped rectangles floated through the white landscape.

Francesca imagined the suspended shapes were fragmented particles of her mother's soul calling out to her from the beyond.

She flashed to an image of her mother, of Terry, in this very spot, this place in another time.

A decade prior, on Francesca's first night in the apartment, her mother had perched on the edge of the table where Francesca's arms now rested. Spine straight, a wine glass extended to her shoulder like a flapper from the twenties, Terry had absorbed Francesca's then-new vista of the Sierra Nevadas.

*Kurt Vonnegut, *Breakfast of Champions*

Francesca had known that the cosmopolitan woman couldn't understand her only daughter's decision to move to the mountains, to the wilderness, so she could research the tendency for gynandromorphism in butterflies of high altitudes. But Terry had flown in from New York to design her daughter's apartment. At least a stylish interior would remind this mountain woman of her Manhattan roots.

The brawny movers in their plaid shirts had looked from Terry's Jimmy Choos to her pearls, then lowered their eyebrows at Francesca's cargo shorts and sweatshirt. Like her, they wondered how these two women could be related.

But Terry had come, and while she'd dragged furniture around the living room, Francesca had unpacked the boxes stacked in the bedroom.

When Francesca discovered the wardrobe box filled with designer ensembles, she'd poked her head into the living room, ready to reprimand her mother for smuggling in clothes she would never wear.

Instead, she'd been captivated by the view of her mother's back, silhouetted by the window, the mountains painted pink by the setting sun.

Like a placid pond rippled by a first raindrop, Terry had sensed her daughter. She turned, disrupting the tableau. Scooting over, Terry had tapped the spot next to her on the table.

She placed her wine glass on the floor, so she could wrap one arm around her daughter and take her hand with the other.

"Once your house is all set up, you'll feel home. Transitions are always the hardest, honey. You've got to go with the flow and know the future will find you somewhere in the present."

Hearing Terry's signature combination of meditation and materialism, tension melted from Francesca's shoulders. She folded her arms around her mother, their heads resting together as they watched the sun slink off to tomorrow.

———

continued on next page...

∞

Fighting the caustic knot that bulged in her throat, Francesca looked out the window, hoping to find the same poetic panorama from her memory. But the snow-soaked mountains were as bleak and vacant as Francesca's blank application.

Francesca picked up her pencil and drew a big "X" across the notebook page. She didn't know what she was going to say at the funeral, but she could work that out on the plane back to New York.

Pushing herself off the floor, she took a deep breath as she crossed the room and knelt in front of her computer. She had to get the application in on time, get her life set up, give the future a space to seep in through her sorrow. Her mother would've wanted it that way.

◆

True Happiness

ADRIANA ROMERO

The Copier

ERIC SASINE

I was standing at the trauma-station copier when the ambulance arrived. As warm sheets of paper stacked into the tray, paramedics burst into the emergency department. A mustached EMT at the front shouted report as they rolled into the trauma room across from where I stood: "Four-year-old female found down by mother after a nap–unresponsive and asystolic at scene." The team went into action. Nurses discarded syringe wrappers on the floor. Technicians and residents hoisted the girl from the ambulance gurney to the hospital pram. Epinephrine was given at the attending's shouted orders. All the while, various staff took turns at chest compressions. As a research assistant, I was just a bystander. I was only there to make copies of research forms. I glanced up as I walked back to my office–the girl's knees bounced unnaturally with the compressions.

I sat at my computer and picked my fingertips nervously. I had only been present at a patient's death once before. A couple minutes passed. The nearby computers normally occupied by doctors and nurses–a dozen stations, maybe more–were vacant. And then they returned, their faces silent, defeated. No one said anything. At last, a phone rang and a resident proceeded with the consult she had been expecting from before. Soon the sound of mouse clicks, keyboards, and a growing discussion between an attending and a fellow brought the emergency department back to its regular pace.

I returned to the copier to retrieve another form I had printed. Curtains had been drawn in front of the trauma room. Dr. L, the attending physician who had led the resuscitation effort, was speaking with a nurse just outside the room. I then saw why Dr. L was still there: behind me, escorted by one of the triage nurses, the girl's mother approached. She had followed the ambulance and had been delayed by traffic. In an instant, I saw that she did not know the awful truth. Though tearful, she maintained good posture and followed the nurse's guidance optimistically. Dr. L, a small and spirited woman I admired, had to tell her. She did so the only way one can: she told her all that could have been done was done, that it was too late, and that her child had passed.

The mother, not much older than twenty, sank against the trauma desk. One of the techs retrieved a rolling desk chair. The woman sat in it, her face the picture of agony–redness filling her cheeks, a pained grimace from which choked sobs erupted in staggered intervals. Dr. L hunched toward her. She cried and put her hand on the weeping mother's shoulder. I grabbed the documents I had printed and walked back to my office, a lump rising in my throat for the woman and her child. Some minutes passed before Dr. L returned to her computer. She wiped tears from her cheeks and returned to charting.

Since starting medical school this fall, I find myself obsessing on virtues and vices in clinicians. While my habits are beginning to form, I feel compelled to emulate the admirable traits I see in others. In Dr. L, I witnessed something that resonated: she did not hide behind professional boundaries. She did not bottle her feelings–she cried with the mother. Some may argue that healthcare professionals ought to maintain equanimity–that to cry is to send patients the signal that the situation is as bad, or worse, than they feared. But at times like this, in which the worst that could happen does, to not empathize is impossible and to not display emotion would be inhuman.

When Dr. L stood hunched over the mother–both women crying–I saw a symbol of the underlying humanity I hope to bring to my career in medicine. Dr. L did not have the lion-proud posture I had seen in oil paintings of William Osler. She did not have the faux omniscience I had seen in Hollywood caricatures of physicians, and she was far from the show-no-weakness bravado I had encountered on the medical school application trail. But she displayed the basic empathy and humanity upon which the finest care is built. As I transition from research to clinical medicine, from research forms to crying mothers, I will follow Dr. L's example.

◆

Dual Diagnosis

LIGIA BATISTA

The patient is a 34-year-old female, financially stable and married.
The patient is well groomed and dressed in a professional, casual manner.
Her tiredness appears to hide behind humble make-up; her speech is
coherent. Her voice is nostalgic yet determined.

The patient refers to insomnia, overbearing sadness, and nightmares
as principal symptoms. When asked about the onset of symptoms, the
patient indicates the present feelings started around five months ago.
Yes, around Christmas time. When asked to describe her symptoms, the
patient shrugs and adds that she does not know. She feels empty. She
gets home and feels empty; she goes to sleep and feels empty. Feelings of
grandiosity, irritability, elevated mood, racing words, and racing thoughts
are absent. Hallucinations, delusions, and disorganized speech or behavior
have not been experienced. Low mood, apathy, low energy, and feelings
of worthlessness lead this provider to believe the patient shows signs of
depression. The patient has not received a previous psychiatric diagnosis,
nor has she previously taken any psychotropic medication. Suicidal ideation
appears absent yet concomitant with mentions of hopelessness and lack
of self-esteem.

The patient is a 34-year-old female, financially stable and married. No
children. I wonder what brings her here today. I wonder whether her choice
of outfit was purposeful: maybe a court hearing? Whenever I ask her about
her feelings of worthlessness, nostalgia, and sadness she reacts–wittily: who
doesn't feel shitty every now and then? Her ability to rationalize every single
one of my questions is astounding and sharp. I wonder if she is happily
married. I wonder why she decided not to have kids. Was it a decision?

Tell me about your nightmares.

They're nightmares, she states. Sometimes I die, sometimes I kill someone;
most of the time, they make no sense. She reassures me that all human
beings have nightmares, that she is not experiencing anything out of the
ordinary. And I agree.

I ask her whether her feelings have been impeding her professional life. She thinks about it for a few seconds. She looks out the window as if looking for the appropriate answer. Outside, the snow falls. No, she said. When she sits down with her patients, not much else exists: she is focused, courageous, professional–as if living in a parallel, segmented, unpolluted system. Her bubble–as she refers to her work–is a safe haven. There, she assures me, she is herself. It is only when she returns home, to that empty home, that she too feels empty. I determine she is not a danger to herself or others and that despite her symptoms she is able to perform her professional duties. My treatment plan includes 20 milligrams of fluoxetine per day, psychotherapy, and regular meetings with this psychiatrist. I remind her that exercising and a good diet is necessary.

The patient is a 34-year-old female, financially stable and married. She does not have any children. Occupation: Psychiatrist. My patient is a psychiatrist.

Can a psychiatrist see a psychiatrist? Would it be the same for me to refuse a psychiatrist fluoxetine, as it would be for a surgeon to refuse surgery? In my assessment, I conclude she is able to perform her professional duties. Did I make the right decision? While she mentions the emptiness of her home and of her self, I think for a moment of the grief of losing a loved one, the hurt that marks one's life despite the time that has passed. Is she depressed? Where do I draw the line between declaring that this woman is sad and declaring she is depressed? Will this medication strip her away from her identity as a psychiatrist? Can a psychiatrist see a psychiatrist?

The patient is a 34-year-old female, financially stable and married with no children, the patient is a successful psychiatrist in pain.

And I, I am the patient.

◆

Awaiting death

JAMES YAROVOY

Though I will finish this rotation
And move on to my next one
I know this is the final station
For you: your death will not be outrun.
You greet me kindly every morning
When I decide at 6 to come
You don't tell me you were crawling
Again through bushes in Vietnam.
Your yellow skin is now your badge
And you keep asking to go smoke;
A few more sunrises to catch
Is all you want before you croak.
You use that word when you mean "die",
You disrespect your own death
And you have never been too shy
To let me know you feel his breath.
You do not wish to fight your fate
You'll never touch your rusty gun
You're too weak, at any rate
To fight against whom nothing's won.
You won't tell me that you want
To reunite with fallen soldiers
Many of whom to this day haunt
You in your dreams, you're seeking closure.
You want your death to wash away
Your sins, your faults, your flaws, your crimes
Salvation you might want today
And punishment you want at times.

◆

Dance with me

WARREN MARTIN HERN

Rest now, little one

MICHELLE ALLETAG

Mt. Evans

DAVID WEIL

rhino Exit

SALLY PRESTON

Berlin

JENNIE HAMMETT

If you are beautiful,
It is with an old whore's beauty,
                    a memory.
                    tired feet
                    open wounds,
          splintered bones showing through
                    like starbursts
                    glowing white.
                    A bright splash
on a grey concrete wall,
a memory of a nickel flung in the air
                    after a beating.
                        ◆

The Last Full Measure of Devotion

ERIC SASINE

Over the summer, I told my friends I would soon be dissecting cadavers as part of my first year of medical school (partly to watch their reactions and partly out of amateurish enthusiasm for all things medical). Whenever I brought up the topic, someone would ask the inevitable: Would I donate my own body for dissection? I gave ambivalent, noncommittal answers, but deep down I was uncomfortable with the idea. The thought of my body being cut into, and stared at, and left in a cold, chemical solution caused me to shudder. I would not do it, I silently decided. There would have to be enough bodies without mine.

So I plodded through the summer with an extra layer of unease regarding anatomical donation. I had a mountain of anxieties in anticipation of that first stroke of the scalpel, and now shame topped the summit. Beginning my medical career by doing something to another person that I would not submit to myself made me feel like the kind of doctor I do not want to become—one who would expect others to behave in a more generous way than himself.

When school started, I stopped dwelling on dissection-related anxieties; the steady stream of lectures, orientations, team-building exercises, and the mountain of anatomical minutiae to memorize pushed all idle reflection from my mind. On the day of our first dissection, I scampered down the hall to the cadaver labs, trying to make sure I had tied my scrub bottoms correctly and running through the pre-lab in my mind. The dissection, like so many feared things in life, proved to be anticlimactic. Along with my lab mates, I incised, reflected and followed directions.

For most of that session, I was focused on completing each step and sub-step of the guidebook. In quieter moments, however, while separating muscles or removing layers of fascia, I glanced toward the cadaver's shrouded head. A weird admiration filled me. I realized I had spent so much time thinking about why I would not donate my body that I had not thought of why one would. In giving her body to the State Anatomical Board, this woman had chosen to help us learn to help others. She had the foresight to imagine the world without herself, and she chose to help it grow even though she would not see the benefit. She chose to shed the ultimate layer of privacy we cling to, the walls of our bodies, in the name of a higher calling. I felt a surge of motivation to do good with my career. Long ago, I memorized the Gettysburg Address, and as I looked at her lying on the humidor a certain phrase resonated in my mind: "that from these honored dead we take increased devotion to that cause for which they gave the last full measure of devotion."

I left that day seeing donation of one's body in a different light. Though superficially unpleasant, donating one's body for dissection symbolizes a healthy outlook on mortality: an egoistic person would not do it—only those who felt genuinely connected to the world would. After death, those who donate their bodies help the next generation learn anatomy and thence medicine, and it is an irreplaceable gift. Although there are now many alternatives to cadaver dissection for students of anatomy (a plethora of apps, textbooks, and models), there is still no substitute for cadaver dissection; no other resource can capture the interconnection and diversity of real bodies.

Now that I have finished dissecting a cadaver, I anticipate being asked that question again: Would I donate my body? The answer would be maybe, but it would be an optimistic maybe—a maybe that says I do not yet have the level of selflessness and perspective to give myself over so completely, but that I hope with time I will.

◆

Body remembers:

MARLENA CHERTOCK

congealing into miniscule form
in a uterus, four limbs,
10 appendages, but one letter
switched in the COL2A1 gene.
An amino acid wrongly substituted.

II
not correctly
how to create type II collagen.
The collagen in joints,
inner ear, vertebrae,
and the jelly of the eyes.

III
growing up scared of retina
detaching, a curtain suddenly
falling down from nowhere,

IV
landing
in Baltimore after a long
flight from Israel, with a cold.
All of these didn't work:
plugging nose and blowing,
yawning, swallowing,
even the nice flight attendant
who brewed tea but tossed it,
pushed the warm tea bags
deep into styrofoam cups
and placed them over ears.
Tears could have refilled
the cups. The next week
body remembers
the world muffled,
50 percent hearing lost.

V
contorting
to fit inside molds
for 22 hours a day
from ages 11 to 13.
These molded braces
didn't stop serpent spine
from slithering into larger spirals.
On summer camp nights,
sweat stuck to skin
and the styrofoam padding
while trying to sleep —
at the front of the tent
a half-broken fan meagerly
sending relief.

VI
laying
in bed
for a week
when back
became a tangled rubber band ball.
Breathing was sharp paper clips
stabbing abdomen.
The tangled clump of office supplies
in lower left back
confusingly tied rubber bands
too tightly around right foot
Losing all feeling in right toes.

VII
autosomal dominant —
the need to survive.

◆

Jean Abbott

Jean Abbott is a faculty member in the Center for Bioethics and Humanities, and a retired Professor Emerita in the Department of Emergency Medicine. She finds it helpful and important to write as a way to reflect on the patients and people in her life, but rarely does this for the outside world.

Fredrick R. Abrams

Fredrick R. Abrams, MD OB/GYN, retired in 1996 after 36 years. In 1983 he founded the Center for Applied Biomedical Ethics. He received a Lifetime Achievement Award from the Center for Bioethics and Humanities at UCHC. In 2006 he was awarded *Isaac Bell And John Hayes Leadership In Medical Ethics*. In 2010, HealthOne awarded him the *Trusted Care Award for Excellence in Clinical Ethics*. His book of true ethical issue stories from his practice, *Doctors On The Edge: Will Your Doctor Break The Rules For You* has been widely quoted.

Larry Allen

Larry Allen is the medical director for the Advanced Heart Failure Program. In between seeing patients and conducting clinical research, he occasionally finds time to dabble in photography. This is the fourth time he has been in *The Human Touch*.

Michelle Alletag

Michelle Alletag is an Assistant Professor of Pediatrics in the Section of Pediatric Emergency Medicine. She completed her medical training at University of Texas Southwestern Medical Center at Dallas, and her Fellowship training at Yale University School of Medicine. Michelle has no formal art training, but has been drawing and painting since childhood. The long, methodical process of oil painting allows for a nice change of pace from the hectic, quick-decision setting of the Emergency Department.

Nasser Alsaleh

Nasser Alsaleh is a graduate student at the Skaggs School of Pharmacy and Pharmaceutical Sciences. He is interested in landscape photography and he practices it as a hobby. As a landscape photographer, Nasser considers Colorado one of the best places for taking great landscape photographs.

Michael Aubrey

Michael Aubrey is Chief Operating Officer for ClinImmune Labs, a University-owned business affiliated with the School of Medicine. He works closely with multiple stem cell transplant teams to optimize donor selection and oversees the molecular histocompatibility (tissue typing) section of the laboratory. His main research interest is the link between histocompatibility molecules and disease.

Ligia Batista

Ligia Batista works as an intern in the Neuroscience Institute at Children's Hospital and is currently a graduate student at the University of Colorado Boulder. She hopes to attend medical school and work as a psychiatrist in the future. Her work has previously appeared in the *The Intima: Journal for Medical Humanities and Plath Profiles.*

Michael Berger

Michael Berger is a 3rd year medical student at the University of Colorado and hopes to pursue a career as an OBGYN.

John Bonath

John Bonath, born in 1951, has had a career as a fine-artist spanning over four decades. After completing his master's degree in fine arts, he moved to Colorado to develop the fine arts photography program at Colorado State University in Fort Collins. After a ten-year, tenured professorship there, he moved to Japan to do independent photo work for four years. Since then, Bonath has been working out of Denver, Colorado. Throughout his career he has received numerous awards and recognitions.

Carolyn Bremer

Carolyn Bremer will graduate in May of 2016 as a Doctor of Physical Therapy from the University of Colorado–Denver. She earned an Art Minor with an emphasis in Photography from the University of Iowa. Carolyn is the "human" behind the *Humans of Denver, CO* photography/social project and Facebook page, and is now endeavoring on a new project called *Humans of the National Parks* (also on Facebook). This is the third year Carolyn has been a contributor to *The Human Touch.*

Carol Calkins

Carol Calkins, PhD is a published author and speaker devoting over 40 years toward her management career in healthcare and higher education. Yet it is through poetry that Carol truly captures the spirit of life's most triumphant milestones and heartbreaking losses. Carol continues to enrich the world with her poetry as she expands her series of Bring Poetry books and HeartPoem novelties.

Marlena Chertock

Marlena Chertock is the Poetry Editor for District Lit and a graduate of the Jiménez-Porter Writers' House. Her poems and short stories have appeared or are forthcoming in *Cactus Heart, Crab Fat, Dear Robot: An Anthology of Epistolary Science Fiction, The Fem, The Little Patuxent Review, Moonsick Magazine, OMNI Reboot,* and *Paper Darts.* Her first collection of poetry is forthcoming from *Bottlecap Press,* 2016. Find her at marlenachertock.com or @mchertock.

Shayer Chowdhury

Shayer Chowdhury is a 1st year medical student at the University of Colorado. Before med school, Shayer graduated from Johns Hopkins University and spent a year abroad studying arsenic contamination in Bangladesh. He enjoys poetry and learning to play the violin in his free time.

Michelle Colarelli

Michelle Colarelli is an Educational Coordinator for the Interprofessional Education Department (IPED) and a Standardized Patient for the Center for Advancing Professional Excellence (CAPE) on the CU Anschutz Medical Campus. She is passionate about team based learning, patient advocacy, and student engagement. Michelle has had other work published in the Human Touch Journal. The message she imparts is to "take responsibility for yourself and the energy you bring to others."

Ryan D'Souza

Ryan D'Souza is a fourth-year medical student at the University of Colorado School of Medicine. He was born in India and lived in several places, including Kuwait, Canada, New York City, Connecticut, and presently, Colorado. He is passionate about the field of anesthesiology. He enjoys basketball and making artwork (particularly glass painting and pencil shading).

Anjali Dhurandhar

Anjali Dhurandhar is an Associate Professor in the Department of Medicine. She serves as Associate Director of the Arts and Humanities in Healthcare Program and as Associate Director of Humanities, Ethics and Professionalism thread. She provides primary care to the underserved and precepts medical students and residents in ambulatory medicine. She edits Letters to a Third-Year Student in the School of Medicine and enjoys teaching and participating in all forms of the creative arts.

Lisa Diaz

Lisa Diaz is a Masters of Public Health student at the University of Colorado School of Public Health. She previously studied Architecture and Graphic Design at Carnegie-Mellon University and at Rhode Island School of Design. Her Women in Business column was published in the *Denver Business Journal*.

Jeff Druck

Jeff Druck is an Associate Professor in the Department of Emergency Medicine, as well as the Director of the Integrated Clinician's Course.

David Eckhardt

David Eckhardt teaches pediatric and adolescent medicine in the Physician Assistant Program. He is a Colorado native and fourth generation University of Colorado graduate. While much of his research involves high tech simulators, in his free time he prefers to be off the grid camping and hiking in the mountains of Colorado or traveling abroad.

Carol H. Ehrlich

Carol H. Ehrlich, Ph.D. is Chair Emerita of Department of Audiology and Speech Pathology, Children's Hospital Colorado, from the U of Denver, wife, mother (3), grandmother (4) and great-grandmother (8).

Art Elser

Art Elser retired after 20 years as an Air Force pilot and 30 as a technical writer. He saw combat in Vietnam as a forward air controller. His poetry been published in *Owen Wister Review, High Plains Register, Harp Strings Poetry Journal, Emerging Voices, The Avocet,* and *A Bird in the Hand: Risk and Flight.* His chapbook, *We Leave the Safety of the Sea,* received the Colorado Authors' League Poetry award for 2014.

James Engeln

James Engeln is a third-year medical student in the Rural Tack at the University of Colorado School of Medicine. He enjoys exploring new places, making new connections, and capturing and sharing his experiences in creative expression. This is his second contribution to *The Human Touch.*

Lynne Fox

Lynne Fox is a retired Anschutz Medical Campus Health Sciences Library Education Librarian. She finds that a balance between the sciences and arts promotes a healthy outlook on life.

Gwen Frederick

Gwen Frederick is the Administrative Assistant in the Dept. of Immunology and Microbiology in the School of Medicine. She's held this position for 18 + years. One of her passions is volunteering with the Rocky Mountain Cocker Rescue that takes in abandoned or unwanted cocker spaniels from puppy mills, abusive homes, and kill shelters from all over the country and finds them loving forever homes.

Kathleen Garrett

Kathleen Garrett is a Research Senior Instructor in the School of Public Heath, Department of Behavioral and Community studies and a Clinical Associate in the School of Medicine, Department of Psychiatry, Behavioral Health and Wellness Program. Kathleen is a lifelong lover of poetry, writing and moon gazing. She plans to continue her research and clinical activities in behavioral science until retirement at which time she hopes to devote more time to writing and spending time in nature.

James "Cal" Geyman

James "Cal" Geyman works as a staff physician for Kaiser Permanente. He graduated from the University of Colorado School of Medicine residency program in Internal Medicine in 1990. Cal enjoys hiking in Colorado's alpine lake areas, and hopes to hike the Colorado trail in the next year. He has published an e-book titled *Colorado Landscape Photo Guide* available at the Apple ibooks store. "

Alexander Ghincea

Alexander Ghincea is a fourth year medical student at the University of Colorado School of Medicine. He will continue his training with residency in Internal Medicine, and hopes to pursue a career in Pulmonary and Critical Care Medicine. Alexander hopes to work in an academic setting where he can pursue his passion for teaching younger generations of student and residents.

Amanda Glickman

Amanda Glickman is a 1st year medical student at the University of Colorado. Before medical school, Amanda worked as a children's book editor and writer.

Ryan Goffredi

Ryan Goffredi is an Electron Microscopist at Children's Hospital Colorado. Ryan is interested in observing and learning about the ways in which small organisms, like cells, can have a tremendous impact, for better or for worse, on a much larger scale. In the future, he is interested in educating and tutoring others. His work has appeared in previous editions of *The Human Touch*.

Oren Gordon

Oren Gordon is currently in his second year of the M.D. program at CU. In his, albeit minimal, free time he travels, skis and reads as much as possible. Most of the pieces he writes are slam poems intended for a stage, but every once in a while a written poem sneaks out.

Jennie Hammett

Jennie Hammett's work has appeared in *The Human Touch, Paragraph, Panhandler, Bullhorn,* and *Chico News and Review.* Black Phoebe, a dance troupe she created with Leigh Kirkconnell, won the first poetry slam it ever entered. This involved the use of zombie costumes. She was a featured reader at Poetry Above Paradise and other old haunts in San Francisco, when poets could afford to live there. She is currently working on a novel, and composing chamber music. She is frequently enrolled in the College of Nursing.

Emily Hause

Emily Hause is a 3rd year medical student at the University of Colorado. Prior to medical school, she attended the University of Minnesota where she received a Master's in Public Health in Epidemiology and Lawrence University where she received a Bachelor of Arts in Biochemistry and Spanish. She's hoping to match in the field of pediatrics and specialize in pediatric rheumatology.

Warren M. Hern

Warren M. Hern, M.D., M.P.H., Ph.D. is a physician and epidemiologist whose clinical practice, Boulder Abortion Clinic, specializes in abortion services. He is Assistant Clinical Professor of Obstetrics and Gynecology and the University of Colorado Denver, Anschutz Medical Campus. He is the author of numerous scientific and professional publications, including a medical textbook, *Abortion Practice*. He is also Professor Adjunct in the Department of Anthropology at the University of Colorado, Boulder.

Michael Himawan

Michael Himawan is a Doctor of Physical Therapy student on CU Denver's Anschutz Medical Campus. His professional interests include interprofessional health care delivery for underserved populations, rehabilitation outcomes research, and education. His solo musical debut—a hip-hop / industrial / electronic concept album called *Six Realms*—is due to be released in late 2016.

Carolyn Ho

Carolyn Ho is a current first-year medical student. Her love for writing began at a young age and has been fostered through her participation in various literature and poetry groups both inside and outside of school. She hopes to continue with her writing throughout medical school and her future career as a primary care physician.

George Ho, Jr.

George Ho, Jr., MD, is a retired Rheumatologist and Palliative Care Physician. He spends his time exercising, reading, writing, doing photography, volunteering, and enjoying wildlife, especially birds. He facilitates a course entitled *Making and Sharing Sound End of Life Choices* for lifelong learners and plans to be a coach in helping the layperson navigate the complicated American healthcare system. He aims to stay active and healthy—physically, mentally and spiritually.

Becca Hollmann

Becca Hollmann is an Electron Microscopist within the Pathology Department and is also finishing her last year of her master's degree in Biology at the University of Colorado at Denver. In what little free time remains between working and going to school full time, she enjoys skiing, birding, backpacking, traveling, photography, art and playing piano. Recently, her first publication was accepted into the journal of General and Comparative Endocrinology titled "Identifying the activation motif in the N-terminal of rainbow trout and zebrafish melanocortin-2 receptor accessory protein 1 (MRAP1) orthologs".

William Jensen

Rev. William Jensen is the chaplain on the inpatient Palliative Care Consult Service at the University of Colorado Hospital. He tries (and usually fails) to find balance between family, work, and self-care through fly fishing and his new found love of running.

L. A. Kahn

L. A. Kahn is an MD/MPH Candidate for the class of 2017. With a background in political work and education, she hopes to combine clinical Emergency Medicine practice with advocacy and writing. Her work *The Life Biologic: Portraits of Disease* is featured at the Hampshire College Library.

Simon Kamau

Simon Kamau is an MS Nursing Leadership and Health Systems candidate (Spring 2016) University of Colorado Denver, College of Nursing. Simon teaches in the BSc Nursing program at the University of Kabianga, Kenya, and is an alumni of Moi University and Kenya Medical Training College, Nairobi. He hopes to work towards influencing health policy and nursing leadership in East Africa. His work *My Conscience is Clear,* previously appeared in *The Human Touch*. His scholarly link is: https://www.researchgate.net/profile/Simon_Kamau/publications/

Karen Leh

Karen Leh is in her first-year at the CU School of Nursing. She previously received an MFA from the University of Iowa Writers Workshop and is the author of a novel *Dream of an Inland Sea*.

Steven Lewis

Steven Lewis, MD is double board certified in OB/GYN and Pathology. He is a Clinical professor in pathology at AMC, where he is also a faculty associate at the Center for Bioethics and Humanities. A photographer since he was 10, he was the first to place actual histopathology findings on patient pathology reports. He has had exhibitions over the last 10 years in 30+ galleries and museums around the world. He recently retired from active practice to teach.

Christine Mitchell

Christine Mitchell has a BA in Liberal Arts, with an emphasis in studio arts from the University of Minnesota. She now attends the University of Colorado, College Of Nursing (Parker, South Campus) and will graduate with her BSN in May 2016. After graduation she hopes to pursue a psychiatric nursing career. In addition to her interest in the healing arts, she has played guitar and sang for twenty years. Mitchell has written about 100 songs and has collaborated with many musicians over the years. During the her first year in nursing school, she managed to record six songs with other Denver musicians. Whether recording or performing, Mitchell enjoys the companionship and teamwork that accompanies playing in a band.

Patricia Nash

Patricia Nash is a Research Administrator in the Department of Radiology She has been painting for over 25 years and her work has appeared previously in the *The Human Touch* and in campus and local art shows.

Ian Neff

Ian Neff works as a clinical research RN at the University of Colorado Cancer Center and is a graduate student in the College of Nursing. His work has previously been published in *Laurus*.

April Netschke

This life is a beautiful one that she is savoring each and every day. She has the utmost passion for traveling the world and exposing its beauty through her Nikon lens. She is a wife, mother of three, nurse, adventurer, rock climber...and most importantly, she is trying to break every mold that the "American Dream" tells her she should be.

Juliette Orr

Juliette Orr is an abstract expressionist who studied at Arapahoe Community College in Littleton, Colorado and at the Art Students League of Denver. She became a mother in 2015 and says it is the hardest and most rewarding job she has ever done. Painting is a creative outlet that brings her great joy.

Leslie Palacios-Helgeson

Leslie Palacios-Helgeson is a 4th year Med student at Colorado and will continue her training as an OBGYN at UCSF in California. Leslie enjoys entertaining her dogs and watching animated Irish films.

Sally Peach

Sally Peach is a 5th year MD/PhD student in the Molecular Biology Program. In 2009, she graduated from MIT, where she received the Joseph D. Everingham Award for her theatrical performances and playwriting. She's been writing poetry since she was but a tiny Peach, and this is her 3rd year publishing in *The Human Touch*.

Huy Phan

Huy Phan is currently a 3rd year medical student who will likely pursue a career in Internal Medicine. In his limited free time, Huy enjoys traveling, exploring, and capturing photos of the people and landscapes around him. In addition to school and work, Huy is also currently in the third year of his "A Photo A Day" project, a collection of photos that artfully documents his medical student life on a day to day basis.

Mary Poole

Mary Poole is retired from Southwest Community Health Services, Albuquerque, New Mexico where she served as Vice President for Development and Community Relations and Executive Vice President of the Presbyterian Healthcare Foundation. Later she worked part-time as Senior Partner for Research for Jerald Panas Linzy & Partners, a fundraising consulting firm. After moving to Denver, she began writing poetry. Her poems have appeared in *The Human Touch* 2014 and 2015.

Sally Preston

Sally Preston, D.M.D. is currently Associate Professor C/T in the School of Dental Medicine. The photograph was taken at Kruger National Park during a trip to South Africa and Swaziland.

Claire Ramirez

Claire Ramirez is a first year physician assistant (PA) student at the University of Colorado. Originally from Arizona, Claire obtained her B.S. in Biology from Northern Arizona University before deciding to pursue a career as a PA. In the future, she hopes to work as a Pediatric PA in an underserved community. In her spare time, she enjoys hiking in the beautiful mountains of Colorado. This is the first time her work has been published.

Ani Reddy

Ani Reddy is a fourth-year medical student at the University of Colorado School of Medicine. She serves as the Class of 2016 Co-President and participates in CU-UNITE urban underserved track. Ani's career aspiration is to become a pediatrician for urban underserved populations.

Romany Redman

Romany Redman is a fourth-year medical student at the University of Colorado School of Medicine. Before moving to Colorado, Romany worked in a Russian tuberculosis hospital and played fiddle in one of the first Irish-pub bands of Siberia. Romany strongly believes in the healing power of art, as well as the phenomenal capacity of folk traditions such as music and dance to create and support healthy communities.

Sharisse Arnold Rehring

Sharisse Arnold Rehring is a pediatrician, Director of Medical Education and Director of Pediatric Education for the Colorado Permanente Medical Group and a Clinical Professor of Pediatrics at UCSOM. Her work has previously appeared in *The Human Touch* and *The Leaflet*, a medical-lit-art-e-journal. She is interested in further developing the role of narrative medicine in her career and the relationship with physician wellness.

Adriana Romero

Adriana Romero is currently a Master's candidate at the Colorado School of Public Health with a concentration on global health and health disparities. She received her Bachelors of Science in Biotechnology and Sociology from the University of Central Florida. After graduation, Adriana intends to contribute to the prevention and control of communicable diseases of importance in refugee camps to enhance the lifestyle of this specific population.

Rachael Ruff

Rachael Ruff is currently a student at Fort Lewis College, studying psychology and forensics. Her mother, Cathy Ruff, is an associate professor at the University of Colorado in the CHA/PA program. Cathy started working at the University in August of 2001. This will be Rachael's first published work. In the future, Rachael hopes to become a published novelist in addition to working in the field of forensic psychology.

Eric Sasine

Eric Sasine is a first-year medical student at the University of Colorado School of Medicine. He graduated from the University of Colorado Denver with a Bachelor's in History. Eric loves spending time with his wife, being outdoors, and collecting rare books. Prior to starting medical school, Eric worked as a research assistant at Children's Hospital Colorado. He hopes to become a pediatrician in the future.

Meha Semwal

Meha Semwal is a first year medical student. She has moonlighted as a tennis camp counselor, existential-crises-haver, and English teacher in Japan. She is a previous Academy of American Poets prize winner for the college of William & Mary. Her writing has appeared on *Black Renaissance Noir, the juvenilia,* and is forthcoming on *Damfino Press.*

Brianna J.L. Smyk

Brianna J.L. Smyk earned a Master of Professional Writing (MPW/MFA) from University of Southern California in 2015. She has published nonfiction work and was lead culture writer for NolaVie.com. Brianna is Editor-in-Chief of *Exposition Review* and the former Nonfiction Editor and Associate Editor of *Southern California Review.* She holds a master's in art history, works at the Pasadena Museum of California Art, and teaches yoga. Find out more about Brianna on Twitter: @briannasmyk.

Elizabeth Swift

Elizabeth Swift is a second year physical therapy student. She writes her thoughts down in bed as sleep arrives sweetly.

Tom Taylor (The Poet Spiel)

Tom Taylor aka The Poet Spiel has had a lifetime devoted to the arts and is an internationally published American artist and poet. His work frequently explores his issues of mental and physical illness.

Heidi Tyrrell

Heidi Tyrrell works in the School of Dental Medicine as a Clinical Instructor and manager of the Heroes Clinic. She has worked in the field of dentistry since 1991 focusing on disease prevention in the field of Periodontology. She composed the poem while living in the Blue Ridge Mountains where beautiful, old wormy chestnut barns still stand.

David Weil

David Weil is the Manager of Operations and Educational Technology at the Center for Bioethics and Humanities. He's been taking pictures since the BC era (before computers), and is a photography alum of Columbia College in Chicago. Since moving to Colorado in 2000 he enjoys hiking, camping, biking and skiing.

Helena Winston

Helena Winston is a 1st year psychiatry resident at the University of Colorado. When not attending to the mental health of patients, she enjoys cooking and hiking with her husband.

McKenzie Winter

McKenzie Winter is currently a second year master's student in Modern Human Anatomy on the Anschutz Medical Campus. Recently drawn into creative pursuits, she is an anatomy, art, and pun enthusiast. This is her first artistic publication. She hopes to continue drawing for recreation.

Matt Wood

Matt Wood is a 3rd year student at the CU School of Medicine. He graduated from the University of Colorado at Colorado Springs with a degree in biology. He is planning to pursue a career in pediatrics. This is his first published work.

Stacey Wynne-Urbanowicz

Stacey Wynne-Urbanowicz is an adult gerontology nurse practitioner student on campus. This is her fourth area of study among philosophy (BS, University of Maryland), geography/cartography (BS, University of Maryland), bachelor of nursing (University of Colorado), so she has been a student for a long time. It takes a special person to teach and share their knowledge with compassion and grace. This poem is about such a teacher that touched her heart.

James Yarovoy

James Yarovoy is a 3rd year medical student at Anschutz. He enjoys politics and reading Russian literature. He wants to spend most of his life in the Emergency Department, but never as a patient.

ACKNOWLEDGEMENTS

There are many people on the team to thank:

- Dr. Robert Anderson, Senior Associate Dean in the School of Medicine, for his continuing support this year
- Dr. Tess Jones, for heading up and promoting The Arts and Humanities in Healthcare Program, which sponsors this and other efforts
- The Editors-in-Chief, Romany Redman and Leslie Palacios-Helgeson, who somehow found the time and energy to bring a year-long effort to fruition, and for guiding the Editorial Board through the process to produce a superb volume
- Members of the Editorial Board
- David Weil, Jack-Of-All-Trades and Manager of Operations & Educational Technology for the Center for Bioethics and Humanities, for going above and beyond to help with countless aspects of this project
- MaryLou Wallace, Program Assistant for the Center for Bioethics and Humanities, for logistical know-how and support
- Scott Allison of Scott Allison Creative for his talent and taste in making this issue a beautiful production
- Bill Daley and Citizen Printing for their printing and production expertise

Many thanks to all!

Henry N. Claman, M.D.